STRENGTH AND CONDITIONING FOR ROWING

STRENGTH AND CONDITIONING FOR ROWING

ALEX WOLF

THE CROWOOD PRESS

First published in 2020 by
The Crowood Press Ltd
Ramsbury, Marlborough
Wiltshire SN8 2HR

enquiries@crowood.com

www.crowood.com

© Alex Wolf 2020

All rights reserved. No part of this publication may be reproduced or transmitted in any form or by any means, electronic or mechanical, including photocopy, recording, or any information storage and retrieval system, without permission in writing from the publishers.

British Library Cataloguing-in-Publication Data
A catalogue record for this book is available from the British Library.

ISBN 978 1 78500 741 5

Dedication
To Beatrix and Evalyn, my gorgeous girls.

Typeset by Jean Cussons Typesetting, Diss, Norfolk
Printed and bound in India by Replika Press Pvt Ltd

CONTENTS

Acknowledgements 6
Foreword by Frances Houghton MBE 7
Introduction 9

1 STRENGTH AND CONDITIONING IS NOT THE EVENT ITSELF .. 11
2 FUNDAMENTALS OF COACHING 19
3 UNDERSTANDING THE DEMANDS OF ROWING 28
4 FUNDAMENTALS OF TRAINING 35
   Chris McLeod
5 NEUROMUSCULAR PERFORMANCE 46
6 MAXIMAL FORCE EXPRESSION 51
7 RATE OF FORCE OF DEVELOPMENT 72
8 MUSCLE AND TENDON MASS 79
9 WORK CAPACITY 89
   Nicole Chase
10 STRENGTH AND CONDITIONING FOR PARALYMPIC ROWING . 98
   Tom Rusga
11 COMMON INJURIES WITHIN ROWING 106
12 TRANSFER OF TRAINING 116
13 EXERCISE TECHNIQUE 120
   Jack Birch
14 TRUNK-TRAINING 151

Conclusion 170
Index 174

ACKNOWLEDGEMENTS

When agreeing to write this book, I didn't quite know what I was letting myself in for. I wanted to share the expertise of some truly great strength and conditioning (S&C) coaches who have been gracious enough to contribute to this book. Many thanks to Jack Birch, Nicole Chase, Chris McLeod and Tom Rusga for your contributions. Several chapters have been shaped by the numerous conversations with Frances Houghton who always reminded me of the importance of conveying the message that we are all human, coach and athlete alike. A big thank you to Paul Thompson for graciously sharing over thirty years of rowing experience and wisdom to add greater depth and understanding of what is most important when working within a collaborative team. Thank you to Karen Bennett, Olivia Carnegie-Brown and Mel Wilson from the 2016 Olympic silver-medal winning British Women's 8 who generously shared their personal insights around the athlete perspective and eloquently articulated the wider impact of S&C coaches beyond that of the weight room.

When I started to build the content of this book, I felt there was something missing, without which I couldn't tell the full story of being an S&C coach. Thank you to both Chris McLeod and Stuart Pickering for being critical friends and helping to shape this book to be closer to the intended narrative. Thank you, Stuart, for sharing your research to help convey the important messages around being an S&C coach.

Several training programmes are included with permission from Chris Boddy. Thank you for sharing your work; it has been great fun coaching you. Thank you also to all those who agreed to appear in the book as models: Max Honigsbaum, Matt Thompson, James Cheeseman and Lu Shi Yu. Finally thank you to Nick Middleton from Nick Middleton Photography, who provided the beautiful rowing images throughout the book. I am grateful to you all.

Disclaimer

Please note that the author and publisher of this book do not accept any responsibility whatsoever for any error or omission, nor any loss, injury, damage, adverse outcome or liability suffered as a result of the use of the information contained in this book, or reliance upon it. Since some of the training exercises and methodologies can be dangerous and could involve physical activities that are too strenuous for some individuals to engage in safely, it is essential that qualified medical advice and consultation is taken before training is started.

FOREWORD

By Frances Houghton MBE
5 x Olympian, 4 x World Champion, 3 x Olympic silver medallist.

PERSON

When I stood in front of Alex I knew he saw a person, not a potential line on his CV. I knew he understood that for me to reach the Olympic podium the time I spent in the gym presented multiple opportunities to improve, and was about so much more than how much I could lift.

I remember one day between sets, he started talking to me about 'normal' stuff – he asked what I enjoyed doing outside of sport. What made me laugh? We compared notes on our favourite box sets.

Becoming Olympic Champion in rowing, getting fitter, stronger and more skilful every day had been the focus of my life since the age of sixteen. In a day that was one like every other – training – food – training – food – gym – food – sleep – he brought connection to the outside world. That day it felt like he reactivated my personality; he reminded me that I was a person outside of rowing. Over time he taught me that the whole of me mattered and the more of myself I brought to my sport – whether it was a Tuesday afternoon in the gym, or the Olympic start line – the more powerful, and fulfilling, my performances would become.

Consistency

During the time I worked with Alex from 2009–16, the gym felt like a safe place, no matter what form I was in. The S&C coaches treated me the same every day – through some of my worst and best years in sport – whether I had just won a world medal, or had underperformed in a major trial, or I was in my third month out crab-walking my way through another injury. It wasn't where I was judged; it was where I could always move forward no matter where I was at today.

Standard

Behind all of this were layers of understanding and clarity – reflecting on what it really took to be a good S&C coach.

During his time in rowing Alex instilled a standard of consistency, clarity, alignment to the end goal, professionalism, individualization within a complex programme, and acceptance of the challenge of navigating strong personalities – that made the rowing S&C programme a gold-medal benchmark of effective contribution. He reformed the impact it was possible to have.

In this book Alex shares those layers – both the technical and the human. He writes: 'Credibility cannot be fast tracked', he's right, and as athletes we often feel like we are putting our 'one chance' dreams in someone else's hands. Our standards are uncompromisingly high.

But Alex raised the bar.

In the End

In the years since I retired, Alex and I have continued to reflect on what played the biggest part in taking me from glimpses of world-class form, but seemingly endless years of injury and underperformance, to standing on the Olympian podium one last time.

He helped me realize that I started out thinking that elite sport was all about winning gold at all costs, and focusing on making myself the best athlete I could be to make that happen, but that for me, my most powerful performances were about far more than my technical and physical ability.

It was really about the connection I had with my teammates, coaches and support staff, and what we could create together – working together to produce something more than any of us could do alone – and being able to share that moment with those people that really knew what it had taken. Not just my teammates, but the physios, coaches, doctors, physiologists, and S&C coaches who had been there day in day out, through the highs and the lows – the PBs and the crumples to the floor. Sharing that journey and celebrating what we had created together was what the ultimate experience in sport was for me. It was, and continues to be, about far more than the medal.

Yes, when I sat on the start line in Rio I knew I was in the best shape I could possibly be in on that day; but working with people who 'got it' and 'got me' not only led me to the most fulfilling experience in my career, but also took me closer to gold than I ever thought possible in that final in Rio.

INTRODUCTION

Accomplishments will prove to be a journey, not a destination

Dwight D. Eisenhower[1]

I feel incredibly fortunate to have spent the best part of two decades working with a diverse array of athletes and coaches in a shared pursuit of accomplishing something special. To be given the opportunity to share my experiences and insights gained during my time working specifically with rowers and rowing coaches is in equal measure humbling and indulgent!

I had the privilege of leading the strength and conditioning (S&C) support for the GB Rowing team for five years, which spanned the London Olympiad and the start of the lead-up to the Rio Olympic Games. On reflection of my time with GB Rowing, this is where I believe I truly understood what it was to be an S&C coach. This understanding had developed from my previous experiences in several Olympic and Paralympic sports, in individual and team sports, and in coaching athletes too. All these experiences have led me to wrestle my own consciousness around what I originally thought being an S&C coach was all about and how I wanted to judge myself, compared to what I now believe this to be and how I judge myself today.

This book shares that journey and outlines what I truly believe is important to be a successful S&C coach, whatever domain you work in. I served as the Head of Strength and Conditioning within the English Institute of Sport (EIS), where I was responsible for the welfare, growth and development of over 100 S&C coaches during my tenure. It was the insights and reflections shared in this book that led to the informed support and development of these coaches. My last role within EIS as Head of Learning meant that I was responsible for supporting and developing the organization's entire staff. The experiences from this role have continually informed how best to support the whole practitioner workforce, regardless of discipline.

Having read many of the emerging texts around S&C, lectured around S&C at undergraduate and postgraduate level and being involved in over 100 S&C coach recruitments, I cannot help feeling that there is a gap between what is taught and advertised and the reality of what happens on the ground every day as an S&C coach. While this book is firmly anchored around the physical preparation of rowers, it also shares insights into the wider practice of being a coach. There is so much more than simply the ability to technically understand movement or prescribe training programmes for optimal adaptation. We also need to understand ourselves, those around us and the context we operate in to truly liberate the greatness in the people we work with every day. I am referring to athletes, coaches and support staff here; we are all human, yet my previous experiences suggest that at times we have neglected the human side of S&C. It is my intention within this text to share real insights from athletes and coaches into just how powerful this understanding is in achieving the desired outcome, regardless of the quality of the intended written programme.

There will of course be contemporary thoughts on the physical preparation of rowers to act as a basis to start providing evidence-based support to rowing populations. A large proportion of what will be shared is built on the experiences I have had before rowing and drawing on some outstanding individuals I have had the good fortune to work with. Some of these individuals have contributed chapters to this book, as they are far more eloquent than me at sharing their experiences and insights. For that, I thank you all.

I have also included personal reflections from rowers and rowing coaches, highlighting a rich perspective that is often lacking within the current literature, with the aim of helping us all to support those around us. It certainly challenged me to answer the questions 'Why do we do what do?' and 'For whose benefit?' Thank you all for your generous contributions.

I hope you find this book a useful resource to help navigate the world of rowing and S&C. I will end with what I normally start with when talking to others around this topic: while a lot of this is evidence based, it is still my opinion and interpretation and therefore my experiences. I invite you to be inquisitive with what you read. If you are unsure of what is written, ask questions and continue to explore until you have greater clarity. Share with your peers, seek to continually iterate your own thoughts and make sense of your own experiences.

REFERENCES

1. Dwight D. Eisenhower (1957). *New York Times*, 17th December (addressing NATO 16th December).

1 | STRENGTH AND CONDITIONING IS NOT THE EVENT ITSELF

The whole is greater than the sum of its parts

Aristotle[1]

INTRODUCTION

Back in 2007, there was a meeting room filled with the S&C coaches from UK Athletics discussing what were thought to be the critical determinants of performance for sprints. The discussion was framed around how much a sprinter should lift or what exercises the sprinter should use. At that time, Dave Collins was the Performance Director. Dave was sitting in the meeting and after about thirty minutes of discussion, stopped us all and stated, 'Stop making strength and conditioning look good, make performance look good'.

That comment made the room silent. It made all the S&C coaches consider what is important for performance, what is used to make S&C look good and to show others that the S&C programme has been successful. The statement 'Stop making strength and conditioning look good' has been a guiding light over the last decade. It is constantly referred to when struggling to delineate what is important and to create clarity around the training process.

The belief in 'Stop making strength and conditioning look good' refers to the incessant desire for S&C coaches to demonstrate the impact the programmes and coaching are having within the weight room with little regard to the wider performance piece. If the focus becomes too engrained around what happens in the weight room, performance will suffer as races are not won based on the load lifted on a bar. The second point being made is the disconnect of S&C coaches defining what is required for performance without regard to the coach and the coach's philosophical model or principles of performance. Each coach will have a varying model on the same event and the way S&C coaches support this will need to vary. The final point being made was how connected is the S&C programme to the coach's model of performance? How aware is the coach of what the S&C programme is trying to achieve and how well aligned is it with the overall performance plan for the relevant part of or the entire season? The S&C programme cannot be done in isolation from the rest of the athlete's programme. If it is, it is likely to be counterproductive.

The key reflections and subsequent questions asked that have guided decision-making while working with coaches are:

1. How can S&C support the event demands?
2. What is the coach's model or philosophy on training for performance?
3. How does S&C support the coach's model or philosophy of performance?

A COACH'S PERSPECTIVE

Before writing this chapter and deciding its content, a few S&C books and articles which were thought to provide understanding around working with sports coaches were read. The texts provided some personal insights into the authors and suggested things to consider and potential opportunities. However not one of them provided a coach's perspective on what the coach feels is most important when collaboratively working together. With that in mind, there was a need to include real coaching insight to share how a coach may view working with others and what is important to consider as a practitioner when working with the rowing coach.

The first name that came to mind when identifying a coach to contribute was Paul Thompson. Paul was the GB Rowing Chief Coach for women and lightweight when I had my first experience of working with him while serving as Lead S&C coach for British Rowing. At the time of writing, Paul is currently the Head Coach for the Chinese Rowing Association and has worked within the sport for over thirty years. Paul was also instrumental in setting up and leading the UK Performance Coaches Association (UKPCA), which aims to support and represent coaches through the professionalization of performance coaching. Paul has been recognized by UK Sport for the contribution and success within coaching through the recognition of being named a Coaching Fellow. Some of the most fulfilling and positively challenging experiences I had were while working with Paul up to and during the 2012 Olympiad. This book is a little better for Paul's contribution.

Some important extracts taken from my interview with Paul are shared here. Commentary around the extracts has been made to provide the reader with greater context.

Performance Backwards

Paul started by explaining the thought process around building performance plans and the considerations.

> ... the first thing needed to have a deep understanding (is) what the competition is and what they (the rowers) need to do in their performance. You need to work back, so you need to be able to plan what physical skills are needed. What tactical technical as well as mental skills, and then you keep coming back to find what are the biggest things that are going to make a difference to the athlete's performance. Because there's always lots of stuff to work on. You've got to work out what your first principles are in your performance and make sure that they're well enough prepared to deliver those things.

Paul is describing the idea of a 'performance backwards' approach.

1. What are the component parts that contribute to a medal-winning performance?
2. How are these component parts developed?
3. Bringing it back to S&C, how can S&C support the development of these component parts?

Having worked with several rowing coaches, each one will have a variation on the model of performance and how this is attained. Where S&C sits within the performance model will also vary, so we cannot assume that a 'one size fits all' approach will positively support performance. While a performance model was not articulated during the interview, having previously worked with Paul while at British Rowing and reconnecting with him at Chinese Rowing, he not only has a model but is able to articulate it in a manner which allows all those that work within the performance support team to fully understand it and how it may be positively affected by the team. To bring this to life, we should look at one of the components; the rowing stroke. While working with British Rowing, Paul articulated the stroke as a 'long, front loaded, leg-driven stroke', which became the adopted approach for British Rowing as the technical model. This is freely available on the British Rowing website.

This model identifies three important component parts that all performance support team members can potentially add value to:

1. **Long:** Distance per stroke is the basis of the rowing stroke. The ability to propel the boat forward as far as possible with each stroke, resulting in fewer strokes being taken during a 2,000m race.
2. **Front Loaded:** The drive phase starts as soon as the blade enters the water. The rower applies force immediately to the oar as it enters to utilize the full opportunity to apply force throughout the early part of the drive phase. The ability to apply force which can effectively be utilized to accelerate the boat can only happen before maximal handle force occurs, which is around the point the oars are perpendicular to the boat. After that point, the amount of force that can be applied diminishes as the boat continues to accelerate. The application of more force will not accelerate the boat any further and may reduce the degree of acceleration. This contributes to the distance per stroke component in point 1.
3. **Leg-driven:** The prime contributor to the rowing stroke is the legs. The technique applied must place the legs in an advantageous position to do this. Chapter 4 provides greater insight into the leg component of the rowing stroke.

From an S&C point of view, there are several areas that can support this component part of the performance model. If consideration is given to the leg-driven component, this provides the S&C coach with a high degree of clarity that most of the force application will need to come from the legs. If this is taken one step further, the drive phase of the

Fig. 1.1 The catch.

rowing stroke is a concentric action biased around the hip and knee being the significant contributors to force application. Therefore, this provides the first positive contribution to the performance model; training methods that develop hip- and knee-biased concentric force application (Chapters 6 and 7 examine maximal force and rate of force development in more detail). When considering the front loaded component, this refers to the ability to apply force early within the drive phase. At the catch (Fig. 1.1), the rower is in a deep compression of ankle, knee and hip flexion. For the stroke to be front loaded, force application needs to occur within this compression position. This provides the next level of insight whereby training methods should bias force application in deep flexion positions of the hip and knees.

A performance backwards approach identifies the critical components of performance and works backwards to identify how these component parts can be developed. As Paul stated, there are many things that can be focused on but identifying the ones that will make the biggest difference is important to create clarity and alignment in the performance support team. The example above demonstrates how important it is to understand the coach's model of performance. Using the example above, not all rowing coaches will have the same model of the rowing stroke so the way S&C practices are applied will differ. Understanding the coach's performance model will inform how S&C can best support the model and the rowers it is applied to.

Paul continued to explain how the performance backward model evolved, which is worth sharing as it provides insights into how long it takes, the iterative process required and the balance between evidence and experience.

> You've always got the textbooks in theory but that always collides with practice and experience. And you know I've been fortunate enough to have a little bit of both. But it certainly took a few years together to get the balance right. And you know when you reflect back over the years you could have done this, you could have done that. But I think they're all learning experiences. I've had the privilege to have some really good colleagues' mentors, some ... from when I first started coaching [that] I'm still in contact with now. But then also the bit of rigour behind it in evidence-based research. And I think if you can combine all of them together and you've got your first principles and when you're trying new things in coaching, if you know that the principles are sound then you can really be confident to move those areas on. If they're not ... then that's when you start to get into a bit of hocus pocus.

The way Paul describes how the model evolves is probably no different to any of us. We find the evidence base to give some rigour behind the thinking but eventually it is the day-to-day practices that become real-life learning opportunities to influence future practice. What Paul articulates are three important characteristics that all coaches – regardless of sport or function – can apply:

1. **Learning experiences:** everything that a coach is exposed to is an opportunity to learn something about what you have done or can do in the future.
2. **Reflection:** to turn events into learning experiences, there is a need for reflection. Reflection is more than a chronological timeline of events but the interplay of coach, athletes, staff, task and environment to name a few important areas. Asking questions of how each of these areas affected the intended outcome and one another will start to provide reflections to inform the next session or interaction.
3. **Coaching is an iterative process:** Paul spoke about getting the balance right between evidence and experience. This

implies that at times either one may have been overplayed. However, you may not know where the balance lies until you have tested the boundaries before finding the ideal balance. This balance can constantly shift, which requires a continued appraisal resulting in the iterative changes in the coaching process and performance model.

Performance Support Team

Paul was asked how the performance support team is viewed within the performance planning.

> I think I guess I'm more of a generalist, so you actually need the specific expertise of people that are experts in those fields. I think it's important to know who's responsible for what but with your support staff you need to be able to at least listen to the ideas and balance those with the priorities. You know, because there's always a biomechanist who thinks that biomechanics is the answer to everything a physiologist will do, the nutritionist etc. So it's about making sure that you can get those ideas and incorporate them into the programme because again it's the number of times the messages are reinforced or the number of exposures people have to that as to how much impact they have in the training. So, you need to be able to work out one of the most important things. And you can't be expected to be an expert in everything, but you can be an expert in the performance, and you need to know how you can bring that together and prioritize it. And that's relying on the expertise of the support staff to bring that into the plan.

Paul brings up that important point within the introduction. As an S&C coach, there is a bias in the way the performance question is being viewed. There is a danger in trying to answer the question from a singular perspective. There is acceptance that there is domain-specific expertise and this expertise can be considered in aiding performance, but there is a need for someone to lead this. This is where Paul identifies being the generalist. Paul is in a position of being the original curator of the performance model so has the greatest understanding of what is available from the expertise surrounding the athletes to apply within the model, and what not to. This supports Paul's previous point around identifying the priorities to work on and not be distracted by everything else that could be done.

The following question was how Paul helps the performance support add value to the performance model.

> In one way it's all about building trust. And often when you're in a team, a young sport scientist may be coming in and promising to change everything and you know you need to be able to get a balance. So again, it comes down to trust that builds up and you can't really gain that until you've been through some ups and downs and built those strong working relationships. Particularly the more time you have in coaching and the more things you see and the direction that you wanted to go. It's understanding what skills people bring.
>
> ... Everybody's got their role and needs to stay in their role. However, you need to have an environment ... where gains can be made in the programme and be listened to. I'm sure other head coaches might do it differently, but I think it works well when those connections happen and there's a bit of excitement about what can be delivered. And so that people are working well off each other.

As with all relationships, there must be a high degree of trust. It is rare that individuals trust one another unquestionably from the outset. Again, with all relationships, there is a need to work on them consistently. The coach–S&C

coach relationship is no different. Paul articulates the up and down experiences that build this trust. The actions and behaviours S&C coaches demonstrate will ultimately determine the level of trust with the coach. As Lead S&C Coach for GB Rowing, fixing bike wheels, carrying boats, driving vehicles on training camp and timing crews along the riverside are not in the job description. However, these were tasks undertaken to support the performance model either by adding value or by removing distractions to athletes and coaches. It is these acts that build strong working relationships, which support collaborative working practices. In the latter years working with GB Rowing Paul stated 'It is my job to prepare a group of athletes, coaches and support team staff to perform one week in every four years.' This profound statement is a reminder that everyone must perform in moments that matter; to do this, there needs to be a high degree of trust across the entire team that everyone will do what has been asked and agreed.

Paul highlights an important point. Having been a rowing coach for over thirty years and evolving the performance model, Paul has a thorough understanding of the sport and what the model is to achieve this. When a practitioner who has limited experience of the sport and may only have a fraction of experience of working within the domain-specific expertise suggests significant changes, the coach will always approach with caution. The chances are the coach may have previous experiences of what is being offered or it is simply not aligned to the identified priorities or does not merit being prioritized. There are two areas to consider:

1. If the ideas suggested are not acted upon, it does not mean the coach is not listening nor understanding what is being suggested. It merely reflects the coach working through the performance model. If in doubt, ask for feedback on the reasons why the suggestions may not have been adopted. Ask for the coach's thinking behind the decision-making. There is often a huge degree of thought behind it.
2. Consider how the suggestions have been conveyed to the coach. Like comedy, timing is everything. Over the years, different strategies have been adopted to provide suggestions and feedback to better land the message. This includes how the message is conveyed. One thing for certain is that email is probably the worst medium to try to do this. With Paul, there would be training camps where rowers would be cycling so there was plenty of time in the support car to share ideas with him. This is where a lot of the progression of the S&C support evolved.

If this is examined a little further, Paul articulated the following:

> One of the things I learned early on as a coach came from one of my coaches and my boss [about how] to change things. So, it's like doing a scientific experiment [when you have] changed one or two things. You know what it is you changed because if you don't really understand what you're doing then your performance isn't going to be predictable. So just being able to take all that in and be able to steer it slowly around. Because if you've got a successful programme you don't want to be going at right angles the whole time because then you don't really understand what you do. You need to have the direction and the pathway that you're going to go in – most of the stuff can be how can you do that better, so that then all the support staff are going in the same direction. So, you need to be able to articulate what that vision looks like.

There is a clear articulation that Paul is responsible for providing the clarity of the performance model, which should provide performance support team staff with the reference point to anchor potential opportunities to. It is also clear that just like scientific experiments, there is a need to only alter one or two areas at a time to truly understand what the impact of these are. Secondly, any opportunities for change should be aligned to the existing programme and not trying to 'fight' with it by taking it in a totally different direction. These latter points are useful considerations when sharing opportunities with coaches. It is important to refer to the questions at the end of the introduction around how S&C can support the event demands and the coach's model of performance. If these are continually being asked, the opportunities for change will be allied to the wider performance model and will be the next logical progression of what is currently being delivered.

S&C Supporting Performance

The next question was how Paul views S&C in relation to rowing performance.

> You never know where those gains are going to come from. Often people look for the ... marginal gains in the sexy stuff. But 95 per cent of your performance comes from doing the basics really well.
>
> And what happens in the weight room must support what's in the boat, not the other way around. And you know at some stage you need to take the time that you work in the gym to put it on the water because it's not just about strength and conditioning.
>
> So, there are rowing programmes that are very successful that don't even do weights. I think that the value comes in the physical preparation of the rower and that you know you need to be able to be flexible enough to get in the positions that they [rowers] need to get into and be strong enough to hold those. You need to have enough conditioning to be able to do that under duress. So, you can do that physical preparation outside of the boat. And I think that's key. And that's before you start getting into how much force transmission you can make in the strength levels etc. And so, for me the key thing is you can do stuff in the gym that you can't do on the water, and that supports water performance.

Paul believes that S&C can support water performance and that some of the work must be done outside of the boat. However, it is also clear that there must be a transfer of weight room performances to the boat. The recognition that some nations do not complete strength training and are genuinely successful competitors suggests there is a need for real clarity around why it would be completed and the impact it can have. Chapter 12 provides a greater discussion around transfer of training. Fundamentally, Paul articulated that if the basics are done well, that is most of the performance model taken care of. However, being distracted by the potentially more exciting marginal gains can have a negative effect on preparing rowers. Ultimately, S&C is rowing training, it is just completed in the weight room.

Final Comments

In the final part of the interview, Paul was asked if there was anything else to consider when working with coaches.

> ... You need to understand performance and understand where people are coming from. Building relationships with the coaches and then building the understanding of the performance in that sport as well. It comes down to the old thing; God gave you two eyes, two ears and one mouth so that you can use them in that proportion and so you need to be able to listen, find out where they are coming from. And even if you think that they're doing some-

thing that is wrong, it's trying to find out why they are doing it because nobody does things to go slower. If you can get that understanding then you can start steering. But if you don't have a relationship with the coach you can't do that. So, the better working relationship you have, the more influence you can have. You have to learn quickly to understand what the key things are. Build that relationship quickly and generally it's best to support what they're doing and then steer them around the corners, where you wanted to go.

There are consistent themes throughout Paul's interview, including the need to listen and understand what the coach's model of performance is and where S&C coaches may be able to influence it. There is a strong sense of trust and collaborative relationships. The greater the relationship, the more likely that there will be an opportunity to influence the programme to opportunities S&C coaches may feel would be performance optimising. Again, the theme of learning quickly and continuously is present. The experiences of working with Paul support these comments throughout and are the themes shared with S&C coaches around effectively working within performance support teams.

Conclusion

The insights Paul generously shared provide real clarity on what is important when working with coaches. While these points may differ slightly from coach to coach, no one will disagree that trusting and collaborative relationships are a good starting point. This will allow a greater understanding of the coach's model of performance, which in turn provides the insights needed to start preparing how S&C can support this model. Without the model, S&C support at best is guessing what is necessary for performance. This runs the risk of being counterproductive through the conflict of performance outcomes. When there is clarity, the entire performance support team will recognize how the domain-specific expertise can support performance and have greater alignment across all this expertise. It is, however, the coach's prerogative to determine what will and will not be included to support the model of performance. Remember it is not that the coach is not listening or understanding. It is more than likely the coach has evaluated the merit of what opportunities exist aligned to the priorities. If the merit is high enough and aligns to a priority, it is more than likely that its delivery will be asked for. If neither of these, it is unlikely that the coach will request its delivery. The prioritization of performance components is critical and incredibly hard to do. It is done to provide adequate time and resource to go after components with real vigour, but also to avoid distraction. If the expertise offered is not followed through, remember it's the idea and not the person the coach is disregarding at that point. There will be other opportunities to continue to support the iterative process of contributing and adding value to the model of performance.

REFERENCES

1. Aristotle. (2016). *Metaphysics* (Hackett Classics). Indiana, USA: Hackett Publishing Company.

2 | FUNDAMENTALS OF COACHING

They may forget what you said – but they will never forget how you made them feel
Carl Buehner[1]

INTRODUCTION

It is possible to pick up any number of S&C texts or read online content and quickly lose sight of what S&C coaching actually is. Having been part of a high performance system for fifteen years, the iterations of what has felt important since joining the English Institute of Sport (EIS) as an intern to the point of leading the S&C team has changed. When starting on the venture of becoming an S&C coach, S&C was not a profession, nor really recognized within the UK until 2003 to 2004. What a good S&C coach looked like was unclear in the early days and has only really started to emerge recently within the UK. There have been clear influences on S&C from the US and the high performance system (UK Sports Institutes) has been influenced by the Australian high performance system too. The high performance system has also inadvertently influenced the wider profession of S&C within the UK. This has provided a unique identity within S&C, which is constantly evolving.

During the period I have been working with British Rowing, there has been an increasing demand for evidence-based practice. All the coaches within the EIS were being (rightly) asked questions around the reasoning for what is done, how did this emerge, how would change be determined and assessed and what the most effective methods were to effect change. While there is a strong belief that there is a need for an evidence base for what S&C coaches deliver, it felt like the pendulum had well and truly swung in a different direction. It felt like there was a stepping away from what was the original reasoning for becoming an S&C coach, or at the very least a reducing of the importance of the act of coaching.

During the early days working within the EIS, shaping what 'good' looked like for an S&C coach was not necessarily a priority, which allowed for a diverse array of S&C coaches, all with a unique way of delivering S&C support. Some were very strong on underpinning knowledge, others on technical expertise and others around the act of coaching. Having spent several years as a fitness coach and personal trainer prior to working at the EIS, I had a strong sense of not only being technically astute around exercise prescription and underpinning knowledge, but also the

FUNDAMENTALS OF COACHING

need to be able to connect with those that were being trained. It became quickly apparent that while self-employed, if the client did not like working with a personal trainer, that client would find someone else to train with. This would result in one less client and less income to support oneself. There was a direct reference point to measure the relationship between trainer and client, based on how long clients would stay with trainers. This provided a high degree of accountability of how trainers treated clients and how they made them feel. The depth of knowledge a trainer had did not matter nearly as much as how much the client felt cared for and how much the trainer shared an understanding of the goals the client was hoping to achieve. This resulted in greater trust and respect between clients and trainers. The observation was that clients made greater progress towards their goals with trainers that they trusted and had strong relationships with, regardless of the evidence base that trainer had for the practices and methods employed. This interaction with clients is no different to working with athletes and has been a strong part of the fulfilment of being an S&C coach. When this part of being an S&C coach felt marginalized, the role was not as fulfilling and left questions around what is really important when trying to be a good S&C coach.

Becoming the EIS Head of Strength and Conditioning gave me the opportunity to address this question. While fundamentally there is agreement that evidence-based practice is absolutely necessary and has provided a strong framework for a lot of the content of this book, it should not come at the expense of the act of being a coach and having strong relationships with athletes and coaches. There is a need for both evidence base and coaching practice to co-exist. During the earlier part of this tenure, a large amount of time and resource was devoted to reinstating the importance of coaching. This included providing opportunities for the S&C coaches to explore coaching and its meaning at an individual level. This allowed S&C coaches to recognize the strengths and areas of development around coaching, in the same way this was available for the more technical and evidence-based components of S&C.

COACHING IS A SOCIAL ACTIVITY

Stuart Pickering, a colleague from the EIS, completed a research project around the key characteristics and behaviours of elite S&C coaches. Elite coaches were those with ten or more years coaching experience working with high performance sport. By understanding what were the elite coaching characteristics and behaviours, the learning and development opportunities for less experienced S&C coaches can be anchored against some of the key findings.

Fig. 2.1 identifies the four key characteristics

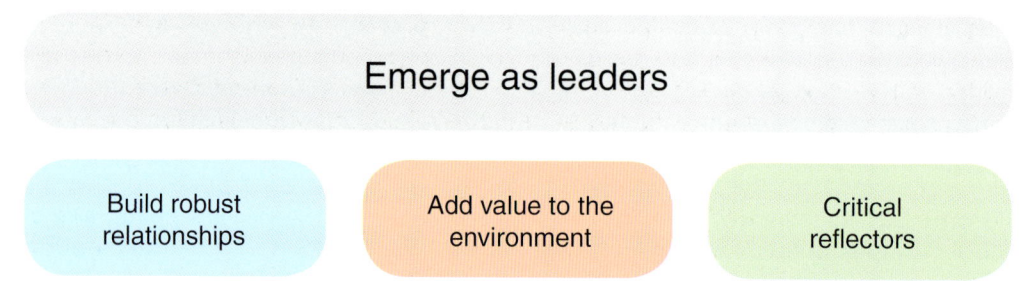

```
                    Emerge as leaders

   Build robust          Add value to the          Critical
   relationships          environment             reflectors
```

Fig. 2.1 Characteristics of elite coaches.

of elite coaches. The primary characteristic is that S&C coaches emerge as leaders, with the three secondary characteristics of adding value to the environment, building robust relationships and being critical reflectors.

Emerging as Leaders

Emergent leadership may be described as those who are able to operate in complex, challenging and unpredictable environments which require the individual to continually evolve; these individuals emerge as leaders and are either given or take responsibility for decision-making.[2,3] Put simply, elite S&C coaches are able to adapt to continually evolving and unknown contexts and are able to make decisions in this complexity, leading others to the outcome of the decision made.

Most leadership definitions include a statement around influencing. Leaders are able to understand the current context and have awareness of the future demands or requirements and can persuade those within the team to take a course of action towards the future needs. Based on the research by Stuart Pickering, emergent leadership is an accurate description of elite S&C coaches. The S&C coaches interviewed all articulated experiences of significant influence within the performance support team and could almost be viewed as lieutenants to the head coach. The influence of these elite S&C coaches went beyond the realms of S&C and impacted the entire performance planning and athlete support.

An important question to ask is how were these elite S&C coaches able to emerge as leaders within their respective sports? The three secondary themes explore this further.

Build Robust Relationships

Building robust relationships covers many areas in which the elite S&C coaches were described to different degrees. Fig. 2.2 provides an overview of the twelve themes that came out of the research. There is no hierarchy of these themes, but a few will be discussed further to provide greater clarity on what is portrayed.

An often unspoken and perhaps uncomfortable truth is that relationships are influenced by credibility. If one side of the relationship does not value or recognize credibility of the other, building a robust relationship will be challenging. Credibility is linked to value and, in this example, the value that can be brought to improving performance. Elite S&C coaches are recognized as having credibility which is growing. Credibility cannot be fast tracked. It takes time to establish this and for others to recognize it. Those who have it will often not view the work or tasks done as building credibility, but simply getting on with the priorities at hand.

Resilience can be defined as the ability to recover from difficulties or as having toughness. This is an important characteristic when working in an unpredictable and complex environment where the only certainty is the uncertainty of performance optimization. It is the ability for an elite S&C coach to continually strive for better, even in adversity. The ability to continually step closer to individuals within a performance support team, or with athletes, knowing that the individual may never step closer, requires a toughness to continue doing it when knowing it is the right thing to do. This is linked closely to not taking things personally.

Management of self refers to the elite coach's personal effectiveness. Elite S&C coaches are well organized. This will often be the basis for dependability. When an elite S&C coach states something will be done, it will be done to the standard required and in a timely manner. This gives confidence to the team and links to the growing credibility.

Seeing others as people first refers to the ability of elite S&C coaches to put role, whether it is athlete, coach or practitioner, secondary to the actual person. Regardless of position or

FUNDAMENTALS OF COACHING

Growing credibility	High emotional intelligence	Empathy	Resilience
Apply expertise at or exceeding expectation	Management of self	Solutions focused	Doesn't take things personally
Direct impact on performance	Sees others as people first	Awareness and understanding of the context	Perform under pressure

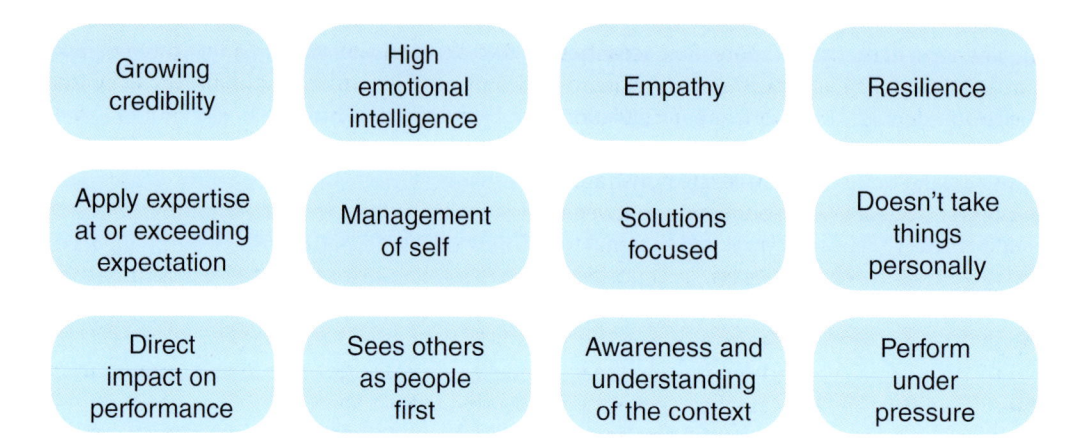

Fig. 2.2 Themes that underpin building robust relationships.

rank, everyone is a person and it is connecting with that person and not the role held where true connections are made. Those in a position of power may be subject to more rewards or perks, but they are for the position held and not for the person who holds it. This is an important differentiation if robust relationships are to be built. Simon Sinek eloquently articulates this point in an Usher's New Look Foundation Signature Event speech.[4] The video clip is titled '5 rules to follow as you find your spark', which is excellent viewing in itself – however, if you want to jump straight to the point, go to 12 minutes, 45 seconds.

Adding Value to the Environment

Fig. 2.3 provides an overview of the nine themes that came out of the research. As with the previous section, there is no hierarchy or order of themes. Three will be examined further to give greater clarity on what is being conveyed.

Social capital is made up of complex factors that contribute to how a group or community operate, including relationships, norms, values and behaviours. It is the network of relationships that allows the group to function effectively. Elite S&C coaches are key agents

Role awareness	Proactivity	Grow social capital
Understand purpose and expectations of the programme, their role and others	Taking responsibility to deliver without mandate	Trust, honesty & mutual respect
Maximize clarity & positivity	Taking stress out and helping others succeed	Perform under pressure, adapt and think differently

Fig. 2.3 Themes that underpin adding value to the environment.

FUNDAMENTALS OF COACHING

in growing social capital. Elite S&C coaches can help to shape the norms and values of the team and can support the modulation of behaviours against these norms and values. Elite S&C coaches have demonstrated a position of being a connection between multiple relationships, internal and external to the performance support team. This position allows for greater collaboration and sharing of insights across the wider team.

Taking responsibility to deliver without mandate refers to elite S&C coaches completing tasks or functions without being directed to do so, but recognizing the impact it may have on performance. Elite S&C coaches recognize and respect the professional boundaries across disciplines, identifying areas that may not neatly fit into a single discipline, but which could be performance enhancing if delivered. This is closely linked to proactivity and role awareness.

During periods of high stress such as qualification or performing at major championships, elite S&C coaches demonstrate an ability to remove stress or 'noise' from the environment. This allows the athletes and coaches to be less distracted. Each S&C coach does this in a different way but all with the same intention; to help others succeed. There are numerous stories recounted of how S&C coaches are taken to competitions or camps purposefully to reduce the stress within the team, allowing the athletes and coaches to perform without distraction.

Critical Reflectors

Fig. 2.4 provides an overview of the nine themes that came out of the research. As with the two previous secondary themes, there is no higher order but two will be explored to provide greater context.

While this is not a definitive exploration of elite S&C coaches, it does provide an excellent starting point to understand what elite S&C coaches do. This can help to guide what areas are current strengths and where time may need to be spent to develop characteristics that may support less experienced S&C coaches to become closer to elite. There is no single characteristic that defines an elite S&C coach, but what is more certain is the idea of emerging as a leader. Elite S&C coaches have a greater responsibility beyond S&C, lead others from a social, rather than a hierarchical position and have significant decision-making responsibilities across the programme.

The research was carried out on S&C coaches working in high performing sport with a decade or more of experience. However,

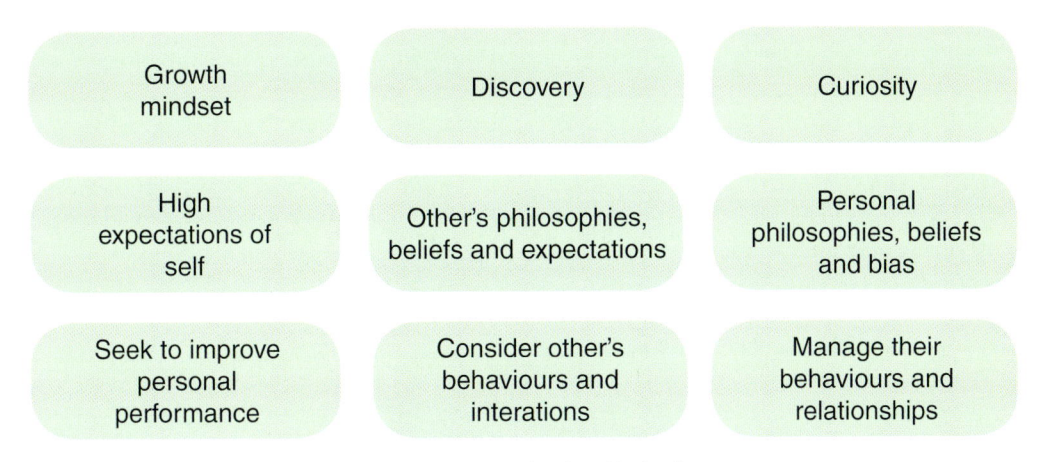

Fig. 2.4 Themes that underpin critical reflectors.

FUNDAMENTALS OF COACHING

the expectation would be this would transfer to others within S&C who have similar years of experience and may be classified as having expertise in that domain (for example youth or school age, special populations and so on).

THE ATHLETE'S PERSPECTIVE

As within Chapter 1, hearing from the people that S&C coaches work with provides the greatest insight of all. While the previous sections of this chapter are relevant and valid, the athlete will be able to articulate what it is like on the receiving end. Within this section, three of the 2016 Olympic silver-medal women's 8 share experiences of working with S&C coaches and what it meant to each of them. There is supporting commentary to provide greater context.

Karen Bennett

I joined the team in May 2015, fifteen months before the Rio Olympic Games. Although I had some experience in lifting, I found it very daunting doing weights with the squad. They were strong and worked at very fast pace, something that I wasn't used to. The S&C would always put me in a group with the strongest girls. I felt completely out of my depth and always asked if I could go in a different group. The S&C coach never let this happen. The S&C coach backed me more than I did in the weights room and knew that I could make gains at a reasonably fast pace. The S&C coach also knew that I would learn from the others and ... had to get the best out of me if I was going to be selected for the Olympics. Without the S&C coach's confidence and belief in me, I wouldn't have progressed as quickly as I did and there may have been a chance that I wouldn't have gone to the games.

Karen articulates how important the confidence shown by the S&C coach was towards her weight room potential. When Karen had doubts about what was possible, the S&C coach continued to back her. The S&C coach provided the platform and opportunity for Karen to continue to grow within the weight room and improve performance, and understood how Karen could thrive by being put in a group with some of the best weight room performers. Not every rower would thrive under these conditions and the main point is not about the outcome of being in a group with the best weight room performers, it is about understanding the needs of the athletes and how best to provide an environment that allows them to thrive. This requires a high degree of empathy. To be able to be empathetic and understand the needs of athletes, the S&C coach must spend time getting to know each athlete. This builds a relationship of mutual trust.

To be clear, when describing relationships here, this is not implying S&C coaches and athletes must be friends. It is implying – as the previous section starts with – a social connection. Without any connection, it will be very difficult to understand the motivations and challenges of athletes. In a previous role, one of the coaches within the team was struggling to connect with the athletes within the squad. After a long discussion, the S&C coach was asked 'Tell me what any of the athletes did over the weekend'. The S&C coach could not answer the question. A further question was asked around 'What do any of the athletes do outside of training?' The coach could not answer this question either. A final question was 'What do the athletes know about you outside of being an S&C coach?' Again, the coach did not have the answer. However, the coach did recognize the point being made. How could a connection be made if the S&C coach did not share anything that was important with them nor attempt to know any more about the athletes? The S&C coach was set a

FUNDAMENTALS OF COACHING

task over the coming month to be more deliberate in seeking better connections with the athletes. Both the S&C coach and the athletes reported significant changes in the relationship, with the athletes stating there was a greater degree of trust with the coach.

Olivia Carnegie-Brown

In 2014 I had a bad year and didn't get selected. I struggled to come to terms with the selection decision and was all over the place in training and in my head. One day in a weights session, the S&C coach asked me if I was OK and if I needed some time to chat through anything, so I took them up on the offer. We sat down after training and discussed what had happened and how I was going to get myself into a better position and an unbeatable position. If the S&C coach hadn't been so invested in us as athletes, they might not have noticed or known anything was wrong and they wouldn't have been able to see the whole picture to help get me back on track for Olympic qualification year. The S&C coach had a holistic approach to their advice and from that meeting, I felt more confident that things would improve. I always felt like I could chat to the S&C coach confidentially about these sorts of things. It's important when training so relentlessly that you have people to talk to and have a good time with.

Olivia describes how the S&C coach was able to see that something was not quite right and how this was affecting Olivia, so they gave Olivia the opportunity to safely discuss what mattered most in that moment. Olivia articulates the trust she had in the S&C coach and how they were able to support Olivia beyond the weight room. The S&C coach treated Olivia as any other human being when observing something was not quite right, by simply asking 'How are you?'

Performance is more than just what can be lifted in the weight room or the time to race 2,000m; it is as Olivia describes much more holistic. When rowers (or anyone for that matter) have good physical, mental and emotional health, performances will have a far greater potential to improve. If distracted with challenges that are not being addressed, this will detract not only from an individual's well-being but the ability to perform at the desired level. Looking at the athlete as the whole and not compartmentalized to a singular part of training or performance will allow the S&C coach to better understand the athlete, what matters most to them and how best to create an environment allowing the athlete to get the best out of themselves.

Mel Wilson

When I was training full time, I found it very easy to lose myself in it. In a world where success and medals are everything, very quickly your self-worth boils down to how well you are performing at that moment. The weights room always felt like a much safer space, where your value wasn't proportional to how fast you had been that morning, or how much weight you were lifting. Maybe it's because I was never one of the strongest people in the gym, but for me it always felt like a space in which you were trying to make yourself a better version of you, instead of trying to beat the next person.

I'm sure that this atmosphere was created by the coaches, who I always felt treated me with total consistency, whether I was on top form, struggling coming back from injury, or just totally wiped out. I'm not sure if it was by design, or just the fact that the S&C coaches are maybe relieved of some of the direct pressure of performance. For whatever reason, they made me feel human again so many times across the two Olympiads. In times when things weren't going well, the weights room had music, encouragement, and made me feel physically and mentally stronger again.

A few months before the Rio Olympics our crew were put under direct threat, and we were facing re-selection. I knew the spot that I had worked so hard to achieve could have been taken from me and I was beside myself. I'll forever be grateful for the weights session that day. Although acutely aware, our S&C coach behaved almost as if nothing was happening. She was encouraging but not patronizing, and in that moment, it was exactly what I needed. I left feeling like I could cope with what was coming. Although the weights room made us physically stronger, it's those things I remember the most.

Mel describes a sense of equality across all the rowers when in the weight room and how the S&C coaches made the athletes feel. Regardless of ranking within the squad based on-water or ergometer training, the way the S&C coaches interacted with the athletes and created the space in the weight room allowed rowers to almost have a 'respite' from the continuous competition with one another. She expresses the feeling of being 'human', which again is the common theme around being treated as a person first and an athlete second. Mel conveys the feeling of threat when faced with re-selection. The manner in which the S&C coach continued to treat all the rowers in the exact same way (with respect and equality) on the day of re-selection and provided Mel with the required support is a testament of how much the S&C coach truly understood the bigger picture beyond that weight room session. The S&C coach was able to recognize the emerging context around the re-selection and how this may affect the rowers, and was then able to observe the behaviours and actions of the rowers, who may have felt under threat, and then modulate personal behaviour including creating the environment within the weight room. This provided Mel (and more than likely the rest of the crew) with a non-judgemental space where the rowers could decompress from the stressors of re-selection. It is clear from Mel's comments, this had a huge impact on how she was able to manage that experience.

All three of the rowers have described the impact of the S&C coach beyond what any job description would articulate. The S&C coach in all three examples demonstrated an acute understanding of and empathy for the experiences the rowers shared. The S&C coach was able to modulate personal behaviours and actions to support the rower as a person, and demonstrated several of the qualities needed to be a successful S&C coach:

1. A wider understanding of the entire training and performance programme.
2. Contextual understanding of how emerging events may impact athletes.
3. Empathy to understand what the athletes may be experiencing.
4. Ability to modulate behaviour and actions based on points 1–3.
5. Athletes are viewed and treated as people first, athletes second.

These should not be exhaustive but are a good backbone to consider when working with athletes.

CONCLUSION

This chapter highlights some key insights into being a coach. There is a need for balance between evidence base and underpinning knowledge with social interaction with athletes and coaches. The research by Stuart Pickering highlights the key characteristics of elite S&C coaches. This provides insights into the areas where elite coaches consistently demonstrate in the day-to-day practices. This is as much about leadership and adding value as it is about the continual learning elite coaches undertake with specific reference to critical reflection.

The honest insights from the three rowers provide real-life examples of just how important the relationships are between athletes and S&C coaches. This cannot be underestimated and shows just how far-reaching the impact of S&C coaches can be beyond the weight room; having a wider view of the entire performance plan, recognizing emerging contexts and being able to adapt to these to provide an environment that allows athletes to get the best out of themselves.

The reason for becoming an S&C coach was more to do with interaction with athletes and supporting their ambitions and goals than pretty much any other component associated with S&C now. As the expansion of S&C has increased and the need to understand and apply more concepts, there have been times when the original reasoning for coaching has become secondary. There are constant risks of this occurring when there are perceived priorities to focus on other parts of the role. The danger is that the act of coaching is perceived by S&C coaches to be secondary within organizations and therefore they may guide personal development away from coaching into other areas. As stated earlier, coaching is a social activity, so requires social interaction. As with all social interactions, time is always needed to develop and evolve it. Regardless of the perceived priorities, the act of coaching should never be deprioritized.

REFERENCES

1. Evans, R. (1984). *Richard Evans' Quote Book*. Utah, USA: Publishers Press.
2. Plowman, D. A., Solansky, S., Beck, T. E., Baker, L., Kulkarni, M., & Travis, D. V. (2007). The Role of Leadership in Emergent, Self-Organization. *The Leadership Quarterly*. 18, 341–56.
3. Smith, B. N., Montagno, R. V., & Kuzmenko, T. N. (2004). Transformational and Servant Leadership: Content and Contextual Comparisons. *Journal of Leadership and Organizational Studies*. 10, 80–91.
4. '5 Rules to Follow as You Find Your Spark by Simon Sinek'. YouTube.com. Retrieved November 8, 2019, from YouTube.com. Website: https://www.youtube.com/watch?v=8l-YpiiBH4o

3 UNDERSTANDING THE DEMANDS OF ROWING

If I had an hour to solve a problem, I'd spend 55 minutes thinking about the problem and 5 minutes thinking about solutions

Albert Einstein[1]

OVERVIEW

Rowers can be found on pretty much any body of water. While training for the Brighton Marathon, the weekend mornings would be used to pound the tow paths of the River Thames through south west London. The view of the river was a mass of club members and amateurs enjoying the sport of rowing. The five years working with British Rowing had a primary focus on regatta distances of 2,000m, which the majority of this book will focus on (although it is definitively transferable to pretty much any rowing event or expedition).

More recently, the opportunity and privilege of working with an extraordinary group of female rowers opened my eyes to what is humanly possible within a rowing boat! The Coxless Crew (www.coxlesscrew.com) spent 257 days crossing the Pacific Ocean rowing 8,446 miles. This challenge tested and redefined how best to prepare rowers for the specific event about to be undertaken. Having learnt to row in 2010 to understand the sport better, I had a greater appreciation of just how challenging it is to sit within a narrow hull trying to forcibly propel the boat forward. The first seven attempts at simply getting into the boat resulting in instantly falling out of the boat may be a record for Redgrave-Pinsent Lake! While the intention was never to compete, when in a single there was certainly a sense of contemplation and fulfilment in the solitude of rowing along the Thames.

Rowing as an indoor sport is also on the rise with specific events dedicated to competing on rowing machines. A former GB Rowing athlete, Cameron Nichol, has created Rowing WOD (workout of the day) to help those interested in indoor rowing (www.rowingwod.co). Collectively, rowing has been identified as one of the top fifteen sports activities completed within the UK.[2]

It is important to recognize that rowing coaches tend to lead the aerobic and metabolic training qualities – I have yet to see an S&C coach lead or significantly contribute to this area. For that reason, the chapter will focus on the more anaerobic components of training and performance knowing that in the vast majority of (if not all) cases, the rowing

UNDERSTANDING THE DEMANDS OF ROWING

coach will lead the metabolic training. For a greater understanding on this topic, *see* Chapters 1 through to 5 in *Training for the Complete Rower* (Thompson and Wolf, 2016).

EVENT DEMAND

Before we can start planning and programming for rowers, it is important to understand the physiological and biomechanical demands of the sport. This will mainly focus on regatta rowing. Regatta rowing is normally competed over a 2,000m course. Evidence suggests the rower will use a mixture of aerobic and anaerobic power.[3] Aerobic fitness contributes between 65–85 per cent to a rowing performance[4] with the anaerobic contribution being between 21–30 per cent.[5] The start of the race requires the rower to accelerate the boat from a stationary position which results in the greater anaerobic contribution alongside the final 250m of the race.[6] Rowers must possess excellent technical efficiency to be competitive, during which rowers will experience a very high physiological demand requiring excellent endurance and anaerobic power.[7,8]

To understand the demands further, a brief review of the Rio 2016 Olympic Games A Finals winning times provides greater insight. Winning times can range from 05:29:63 (men's coxed 8) to 07:21.54 (women's single scull). Table 3.1 provides details of the winning times at the 2016 Rio Olympics demonstrating the breadth of time taken to complete 2,000m across different boat classes. These times are clearly influenced by several factors. Sex (male or female), crew number (single sculls to coxed 8s), competition classification (lightweight or openweight), and sweep rowing (single oar per rower) or sculling (two oars per rower) will all influence the speed of a boat.[9] Environmental factors will also contribute to the rowing performance. Wind speed, wind direction, water depth, water temperature, water current and air temperature will all impact on the degree of drag during racing by influencing the amount of water and air resistance.[10,11,12]

While the distance of competition remains at 2,000m, the amount of diversity between

Table 3.1 Boat classes and winning times at the 2016 Rio Olympics

Boat Class	Code	Winning Time
Lightweight Women's Double Sculls	LW2x	07:04.7
Women's Single Sculls	W1x	07:21.5
Women's Coxless Pair	W2-	07:18.3
Women's Double Sculls	W2x	07:40.1
Women's Quadruple Sculls	W4x	06:49.3
Women's Coxed Eight	W8+	06:01.5
Lightweight Men's Double Sculls	LM2x	06:30.7
Lightweight Men's Coxless Four	LM4-	06:20.5
Men's Single Sculls	M1x	06:41.3
Men's Coxless Pair	M2-	06:59.7
Men's Double Sculls	M2x	06:50.8
Men's Coxless Four	M4-	05:58.6
Men's Quadruple Sculls	M4x	06:06.8
Men's Coxed Eight	M8+	05:29.6

(LW: Lightweight Women, W: Women, LM: Lightweight Men, M: Men, x: Sculling, -: Coxless, +: Coxed)

UNDERSTANDING THE DEMANDS OF ROWING

boat class, type of rowing (sweep rowing or sculling) and body mass of rowers makes the event demand slightly different for each crew. This is what makes preparing rowers for competition so exciting.

ATHLETE DEMANDS

Understanding the mechanical demands will start to influence the physical preparation requirements for rowers. This has influenced the subsequent chapters in terms of the force application requirements for rowers to be able to meet the demands of competitive rowing. It is worth noting that up to this point, it has been difficult to accurately measure mechanical demands of rowing in the boat itself. While there is evidence that has increased in recent times, some of the evidence is collected using rowing ergometers (Concept2 ergometers). While this is not a direct measure of on-water performance, it is a good proxy for this and inferences around performance can be made to rowing populations.

When examining the first ten strokes on a rowing ergometer, estimated peak handle forces were recorded as 1,352 newtons (N) for males and 1,019N for females.[13] This has been supported with measurements of on-water racing of male single scullers who recorded peak forces of between 1,000–1,500N within the first ten seconds of the race.[14]

The biggest impact strength training can have on rowing performance has been demonstrated to be at the start of the race.[15] The largest forces have been measured at the start[16], most likely due to the need to rapidly accelerate a stationary boat up to race speed and stroke rate.[17] While the peak forces demonstrated at the start of the race may be momentary, the rowers are able to maintain an impressive 65–70 per cent of this force production through the remainder of the competition distance.[18]

On average, rowers will take 220 to 250 strokes over 2,000m.[19] Rowing economy is an important component of performance.[20] There is evidence that stronger rowers (those that can produce greater force productions) are more economical than weaker rowers.[21]

Ergometer power strokes are a training or testing method whereby a small number of maximum effort stroke repetitions are completed, starting with a stationary ergometer flywheel.[22] This can be used to measure peak rowing ergometer power. Interestingly, there is evidence that 92 per cent of 2,000m rowing ergometer performance can be accounted for by the rowers' peak rowing ergometer power[23], demonstrating again the need for rowers to be high force producers during the limited time of the drive phase (Figs 3.1 and 3.2). Supporting evidence demonstrated that rowing ergometer peak power can also predict rowing 2,000m performance alongside several other aerobic performance metrics.[24]

When on water, power has been measured at the oar, the measurements have been as high as 450–550 watts.[25] The on-water largest forces observed during the rowing stroke are just after the catch (oar or rowing machine handle nearly perpendicular to the boat) during the initial drive phase.[26] Figs 3.1–3.3 highlight the catch and maximal handle force position. The leg drive is the primary contributor to this force production.[27] There has been some research to determine the contribution to rowing power by body segments. The legs contribute 46 per cent, the trunk contributes 31 per cent and finally the arms contribute 23 per cent of the rowing power.[28] The research dives a little deeper in understanding the utilization of each of those segments' maximum capacity which gives another insight into potential physical preparation requirements for the rower. The legs utilize 95 per cent of their maximum capacity, the trunk 55 per cent and the arms 75 per cent.[29] There is also evidence that rowers will use approximately 70 per cent of their total body mass to help

UNDERSTANDING THE DEMANDS OF ROWING

the acceleration of the boat.[30] Based on this evidence, rowing is a whole body movement. Rowing is a highly coordinated movement utilizing the whole body to link the force production from the leg drive, through the trunk to then apply force to the oar handles.[31] The time a rower has to apply force during the rowing stroke is both rate (time) and distance (length of stroke) constrained, meaning rowers are required to produce large forces during short periods of time.[32] Figs 3.1–3.3 highlight the key positions during the drive phase of the rowing stroke:

1. **The catch:** the point at which the blade enters the water.
2. **Maximal handle force:** the point at which the peak force measured during the rowing stroke occurs (blade almost perpendicular to the boat).
3. **Extraction:** the point at which the drive phase ends, and the blades are removed from the water.

The distance between the oar entering the water during Fig. 3.1 and reaching maximal handle force in Fig. 3.2 is very small. This further strengthens the need of a rower to produce a high degree of force in a constrained timeframe.[33] It is during the drive phase that the greatest forces are produced to accelerate the boat.[34]

Fig. 3.1 The catch of the drive phase.

Fig. 3.2 Maximal handle force of the drive phase.

UNDERSTANDING THE DEMANDS OF ROWING

Fig. 3.3 Extraction at the end of the drive phase.

The evidence above demonstrates the need for the rower to produce maximal and repeatable force production for continuous periods of time throughout the race. Force and power measurements have also been demonstrated to have a relationship with 2,000m performance.[35,36] When starting to look specifically at the relationship of strength training to 2,000m performance, there is good evidence as well as personal experiences of this. Maximum bench pull and leg press performance have been correlated to rowing performance.[37] As highlighted previously, strength training can have a significant effect on the start of the race.[38] Rowing economy can also be developed through strength training, with stronger rowers having greater rowing economy than weaker rowers.[39] When comparing those who are strong and weak, those who are stronger have better anaerobic capacities, have a greater fatigue resistance so have a greater potential to be more economical compared to their weaker counterparts.[40] Rowers and rowing coaches alike will agree this is advantageous as for the same workload, the metabolic demand will be less.[41] This should allow for rowers to either complete a little more training or slightly increase the training intensity as their economy increases or more importantly transfer this economical rowing to competition. The evidence is compelling enough to ensure that strength training is a component within the rower's training programme, knowing the benefits it can have on performance.

As described earlier, the ability to generate a large amount of force to propel the boat more quickly than the competitor's while sitting in a narrow hull is a great skill. This is what separates good and excellent rowers. The whole body coordination and contribution to the rowing stroke places greater demand and complexity on preparing rowers to compete. Rowers are highly trained endurance athletes who are capable of producing very large forces during limited timeframes, a strength which is developed through extensive resistance training. It is not uncommon to have open-weight male rowers being a lean 100kg or greater with exceptional aerobic and anaerobic capabilities. Finding this balance is the fine symmetry between the art and science of S&C!

INTEGRATING STRENGTH TRAINING

It is important to note that most, if not all, rowing coaches plan and programme for the majority of aerobic and anaerobic training rowers complete. Whether this is on or off the water, the rowing coach is in prime position to programme for the entire training structure. As already discussed in Chapter 1, it is absolutely imperative that S&C training does not sit separate to the rest of the programme. As already demonstrated, the impact of strength training can be huge. Having a single agreed, understood and shared programme of physical preparation that includes every aspect of training will be optimal for training adaptation. It will also avoid duplication or maladaptation. The S&C coach is in an ideal position to help inform the coaches (and athletes and support staff) of training demands and rowers' responses to support coaches with their decision-making around the wider programme.

The biggest mistake I have made or observed is when the S&C coach develops a programme in isolation to the rest of the programme. It is the rower that will ultimately suffer as there are competing training stimuli that are not aligned and it is therefore suboptimal. It is likely to also cause frustration for both the coach and S&C coach. Understanding the purpose of the training block and how strength training sits within it will create a more aligned programme, where the rower will benefit from this alignment of a unified training purpose.

REFERENCES

1. Couger, D. J. (1995). *Creative Problem Solving and Opportunity Finding (Decision-making and Operations Management).* Massachusetts, USA: Boyd & Fraser Publishing Company.
2. Thompson, P., & Wolf, A. (2015). *Training for the Complete Rower: A guide to improving your performance.* Wiltshire, UK: The Crowood Press.
3. Mäestu, J., Jürimäe, J., & Jürimäe, T. (2005). Monitoring of Performance and Training in Rowing. *Sports Medicine.* 35, 597–617.
4. Droghetti, P. K., & Nilsen, T. (1991). The Total Estimated Metabolic Cost of Rowing. *FISA Coach.* 2, 1–4.
5. Secher, N. H. (1975). Isometric Rowing Strength of Experienced and Inexperienced Oarsmen. *Medicine & Science in Sport.* 7, 280–83.
6. Secher, N. H. (1993). Physiological and Biomechanical Aspects of Rowing: Implications for training. *Sports Medicine.* 15, 24–42.
7. Mäestu *et al.* (2005).
8. Nevill, A. M., Allen, V. S., & Ingham, S. A. (2011). Modelling the Determinate of 2000m Rowing Ergometer Performance: A proportion, curvilinear allometric approach. *Scandinavian Journal of Medicine & Science in Sport.* 21, 73–78.
9. Ingham, S. A., Whyte, G. P., Jones, K., & Nevill, A. M. (2002). Determinants of 2000m Rowing Ergometer Performance in Elite Rowers. *European Journal of Applied Physiology.* 88, 243–46.
10. *Ibid.*
11. Mäestu *et al.* (2005).
12. Neville *et al.* (2011).
13. Hartman, U., Mader, A., Wasser, K., & Klauer, I. (1993). Peak Force, Velocity, and Power During Five and Ten Maximal Rowing Ergometer Strokes by World Class Female and Male Rowers. *International Journal of Sports Medicine.* 14 (Suppl. 1), S42–S45.
14. Steinacker, J. M. (1993). Physiological Aspects of Training in Rowing. *International Journal of Sports Medicine.* 14, 3–10.
15. Lawton, T. W., Cronin, J. B., & McGuigan, M. R. (2011). Strength Testing and Training of Rowers: A review. *British Journal of Sports Medicine.* 41, 413–32.
16. Steinacker (1993).
17. Lawton *et al.* (2011).
18. Steinacker (1993).
19. Secher (1993).
20. Bourdin, M., Messonnier, L., Hager, J. P., & Lacour, J. R. (2004). Peak Power Out-

21. Ibid.
22. Ingham (2002).
23. Bourdin *et al.* (2004).
24. Ingham (2002).
25. Steinacker (1993).
26. Schwanitz, P. (1991). Applying Biomechanics to Improve Rowing Performance. *FISA Coach.* 2, 1–7.
27. Ibid.
28. Klesnev, V. (1991). Improvement of Dynamical Structure of the Drive in Rowing. PhD Thesis. Saint-Petersburg Institute of Sport.
29. Ibid.
30. Ingham (2002).
31. Lawton *et al.* (2011).
32. Thompson & Wolf (2015).
33. Ibid.
34. Ibid.
35. Ingham (2002).
36. Steinacker (1993).
37. Izquierdo-Gabarren, M., Txabarri-Exposito, R. G., Villarreal, E. S., & Izquierdo, M. (2010). Physiological Factors to Predict on Traditional Rowing Performance. *European Journal of Applied Physiology.* 108, 83–92.
38. Lawton *et al.* (2011).
39. Bourdin *et al.* (2004).
40. Stone, M. H., Stone, M. E., Sands, W., Pierce, K. C., Newton, R. U., Haff, G. G., & Carlock, J. (2006). Maximum Strength and Strength Training – A relationship to endurance? *Strength and Conditioning Journal.* 28, 44–53.
41. Ibid.

(put Predicts Rowing Ergometer Performance in Elite Male Rowers. *International Journal of Sports Medicine.* 25, 368–73.)

4 | FUNDAMENTALS OF TRAINING

Chris McLeod

You never change things by fighting the existing reality. To change something, you build a new model that makes the existing model obsolete

Buckminster Fuller[1]

INTRODUCTION

The process of training can first and foremost be seen as a 'creative' act, with creativity being defined as the 'newness that is useful'. For something to be 'useful' in the training context one or both conditions below must be met:

- Training produces a positive change in the individual that enhances sports performance.
- Training produces insight that positively impacts future training.

The purpose of any training programme can therefore be seen as:

> To produce a positive change in sports performance and create insight that positively affects the training process moving forwards.

This chapter will not describe the specifics of training but will aim to address three fundamental questions that underpin the purpose described above:

1. What do we believe about training as a creative act?
2. What can we change about 'sports performance'?
3. What is insight and how is it created?

While none of the information in this chapter is 'new' and it could be argued it has been described in multiple forms previously, the intention is to provide a framework that more adequately allows practitioners and coaches to explore new and novel ways of looking at training to ensure a more individual, specific, performance-focused and insight-generating outcome.

WHAT IS BELIEVED ABOUT TRAINING AS A CREATIVE ACT?

In order for us to see training as a creative task we first must acknowledge its complexity. For a creative solution to be required the coach must first acknowledge that:

FUNDAMENTALS OF TRAINING

- The desired outcome is not 100 per cent clear and may be subject to change.
- There is uncertainty in the best way to achieve this.
- The 'response' cannot be guaranteed and is heavily dependent on context.
- It is influenced by personal relationships and group dynamics.

While many texts and training models explicitly or implicitly imply that the act of training is linear, predictable and controllable, the reality of both training research and experiences of day-to-day training point in the opposite direction.

Examples of this include:

- The range of individual response to the same training response.
- The effect of training context/environment on adaptation.
- Exceptional sports performances seen when the 'data' and/or coach intuition would suggest that this should not be the case.

The major challenge to acknowledging the complexity of the process is what is known as *retrospective coherence*. This is where a successful outcome 'makes sense' when you look back over the process. An example of this is when sports teams are in conflict and in the moment the coach experiences panic and fear that it is all going wrong, but three months later when the team have won a major championship, the message is that it was all part of the plan, the conflict was needed to take the team to higher levels. While this may be the case, the feelings, decision-making, and clarity are very different in the moment versus when looked back at over a period of time. This confidence after the event can give the individual and/or group a sense that it all makes sense and the planning was always in place. Most of the time however this confidence and coherence is only apparent after the event, and at the time there was a high level of uncertainty and doubt. It may be the case that the acknowledgment of this doubt, balanced with enough confidence and certainty to allow decisions to be made, raises the potential for increased insight through the appreciation of coaching as a creative act.

WHAT CAN BE CHANGED ABOUT SPORTS PERFORMANCE?

Changing How People Move: The Stability/Variation Paradox

While much has been written about the challenge of transfer, the reality in day-to-day coaching is that this process should be anchored in a shared understanding of what performance changes are required by the coach, S&C coach and the entire performance support team. To satisfy the principles of

> **THE SHARED UNDERSTANDING TEST**
>
> A 'simple' test for any performance team is that if each person was locked in a room and had to answer the questions below, how consistent the answers would be:
>
> - Describe the performance goal for the athlete/team.
> - For this to be achieved:
>   - What would you be able to see the athlete doing in performance that they don't do now?
>   - What needs to change in the data?
>   - What would the coach/athlete say that they are not seeing now?
>   - What do you believe are the biggest non-negotiables in achieving this?
>   - How will you know you are making progress?

complexity, this shared understanding does not need to be 'right' but coherent. In this context coherence means that it makes sense and fits with the context. This coherence can be tested by exploring these three fundamental questions:

1. Does it fit with the facts?
2. Is the plan logical?
3. Will it have impact in the real world?

The conversations that occur around the training process are hugely influenced by the lens through which individuals and teams view training. One interesting way to view training is that in order to influence performance we must change the way that an athlete moves. It could be argued that to create any change in sports performance something must change about the way the athlete moves:

- For high force/rate of force training to be seen as effective it must change the way that the athlete performs their sport-specific movement.
- For many forms of endurance training the desired outcome is to perform a particular movement for a longer period of time.
- For injury prevention training, the higher-level goal is to change the way an athlete moves to create a more 'effective and safe' movement pattern. Even something as simple as 'glute activation' exercises are underpinned by an assumption that this increased 'activation' will improve activation in context and presumably positively influence internal rotation of the femur and knee while increasing the body's ability to absorb and utilize force.

The unintended positives of this focus on changing movement related to performance are that:

1. It allows the coaches to describe what they want to see change and why, while challenging this allows others to explore and understand the coach's implicit tacit knowledge, how they view sports performance, what is important to them and why.
2. It takes us away from the training method (this is expanded upon in the next chapter) and creates a consistent view of what success would look like.
3. It automatically creates a platform for integrated support due to the fact that how someone moves in context is influenced by aspects such as:
   - Socio-culture
   - Physicality
   - Psychology
   - Context
   - Coaching behaviour.

To further explore this and create a platform to discuss how we change movement, we must unpick what we believe about movement and how this may affect the training process.

There are many different definitions of what optimal movement is but broadly it can be described as the ability to 'perform the right movement at the right time that positively affects the performance goals'. A shared understanding of what this means in context is essential for the most effective and integrated performance planning/programming.

COACHING QUESTIONS

- If the training programme is successful what changes in movement would be expected to be seen in the athlete's performance context?
  Describe this pre- and post-change; as if someone else were watching it on TV and had to explain it to a young child.

FUNDAMENTALS OF TRAINING

One interesting concept that may add value to how we view human movement development is the stability/variation balance. This is underpinned by some key principles that we will explore in more depth:

1. Elite performers display great consistency (high stability) in parts of the movement that are crucial to performance – essential positions or 'anchors'.[2]
2. Elite performers display 'high' variability in their ability to get to these 'essential positions'.[3]
3. Elite performers coordinate their body in a way that allows the two principles above to occur and is consistent with anatomical principles.

An example of these playing out can be seen during a single rowing stroke:

1. Expert performers display great consistency in parts of the movement that are essential to success, the catch position (anchors).
2. Expert performers display 'high' variability in the movement path in and out of the catch position.[4]
3. Expert performers have the ability to create appropriate 'trunk' tension during the end of the drive phase. This means that the trunk can work in an 'isometric' fashion that fits with its architecture, which means it can effectively transfer force from lower to upper body and creates stability in the system when it is required (this can be contrasted with the instability created if that 'trunk' is trying to contract concentrically which would mean that it would not be working in line with its architecture, could not most effectively transfer force and would create huge amounts of variation/instability at a crucial part of the rowing stroke).

This low variation in positions that are essential to performance and 'high' variation in ability to get in and out of them brings with it a number of potential advantages for the human body and performance:

1. Allows consistency in performance under a variety of conditions.
2. Allows the body to cope with perturbations through this ability to 'find' positions that matter in a consistent way, such as changes in weather, fatigue, and stress.
3. Decreases injury risk. Research has shown that the body's ability to produce high variability around these positions of stability means that structures can be off-loaded when there are low levels of pain and/or potential injury, essentially the body can 'search' for alternative solutions on a micro and macro scale.[5,6,7]
4. The ability to maintain this stability/variation balance has also been shown to aid learning and retention as the body can more effectively search for new and novel solutions to a new movement task.[8,9,10]

A full review of this balance between stability and variability is outside of the realms of this article but the key areas that will help us explore the implications of this in the next chapter are:

- **The body's structure is a rate limiter to specific movement solutions emerging.** A specific example of this is described by Thelan when looking at babies beginning to walk.[11] Effective walking involves key reflexes (such as flexion/extension reflex). Her research showed that while these were not present in many babies when the baby was 'de-loaded', these reflexes emerged. The hypothesis was that the rate limiter was the baby's weight, as they did not have the required force-generating ability to offset this and utilize the inherent reflexes. This has huge implications for

FUNDAMENTALS OF TRAINING

strength training and also for understanding the developing and growing athlete.
- **Learning environments.** The research that underpins the concepts above shows that adequate variability in training enhances learning, performance adaptability and reduces injury risk. This variability needs to be balanced with adequate specificity, reward and 'intensity'.[12,13,14,15,16]

Specific to rowing this would mean that training should be targeted at creating environments that:

1. Encourage the athletes to find and repeat the positions that are known to underpin performance.
2. Expose them to adequate variation to enhance learning and the athlete's ability to find the positions and perform the movement consistently, regardless of perturbations/change.
3. Develop the structure required to optimize both training and ability to be strong in positions that matter.

COACHING QUESTIONS
- What are the key positions/variables that underpin success in rowing/with your athlete?
- Where are the rowers now and what changes would be expected to be seen?

Positively Affecting Optimal Movement: Structure versus Coordination

While the conceptual framework above gives an interesting lens to view human movement, from a coaching perspective we are still left with the 'So what?' question. In order to address the 'So what?' question, there is a need to address the current state.

The purpose of training is to produce a positive change in sports performance and create insight that positively affects the training process moving forwards. Specifically, this means increasing the athlete's ability to perform the right movement at the right time by allowing them to be more consistent in the key positions and have increased flexibility getting in how the athletes finds them.

In order to achieve this, the training of the individual is to contract a muscle(s) hard enough, quickly and at the right time.

For example, when an athlete throws a javelin, the musculature must contract hard enough, quickly enough and at the right time against the internal and external yielding forces that are placed across each joint to release the javelin at the right velocity, angle and height.

The two major areas that we can change to affect this are:

1. Changes in structural qualities that are beneficial to the specific task.
2. Neural activation of the muscle that is specific to the outcome task.

While these two statements are not new to many coaches, the reality of them and how they underpin training programmes are crucial and are a huge area for exploration.

Creating Change

In designing and implementing training solutions the complex nature of the process means that many different methods may be successful, however the process should be driven by aiming to make the 'optimal' difference and by choosing methods that are most aligned to the outcome task and training purpose. This is the context in which coaches aim to address the two areas stated above that must be delivered to create change.

FUNDAMENTALS OF TRAINING

The Countermovement Jump Challenge: Expression vs Development

If it is believed that for changes to be made in human movement, we must create change in structural qualities that are beneficial to the outcome task and/or neural activation specific to the outcome task[17], there is a coaching challenge based around which exercises are optimal to achieve these outcomes. To explore this, a low-load countermovement jump will be used as an example (with the outcome task as acceleration) and within the context of making changes in these two specific areas.

The potential adaptations for the countermovement jump (not exhaustive) are:

- Increase rate coding.
- Synchronization and motor unit recruitment.
- Decrease pre-/post-synaptic inhibition.
- Possible increased tendon type III collagen turnover.

If these are placed on a potential spectrum based on the two primary training outcomes it may look like Fig. 4.1.

What this small task shows is that there are very few adaptations that coaches can be very confident in that meet the two major criteria described above. While a few can be inferred there can be little confidence that this is the case. While much research has described the strong correlation between exercises such as the countermovement jump and sprint performance, there is a chance that the level of certainty derived from these is clouded by misinterpreting correlation for causation and presuming upwards causation.

Correlation Versus Causation

There are many similarities in the major muscle groups used and some kinematic and kinetic variables of acceleration and jumps squats. It is therefore logical that there is likely to be a correlation between the two tasks. This does not however mean that improvements in countermovement jumps have a causal effect on acceleration ability. This is made even clearer by the reality portrayed in Fig. 4.2.

This leads us to explore the concept of upwards causation. Upwards causation assumes that changes lower down a continuum affect those higher up. This can best

Structural changes that are beneficial to the outcome task	Changes that are specific to the training task	Neural changes specific to the outcome task
Possible increased tendon type III collagen turnover	Increase rate coding, synchronization and motor unit recruitment Decrease pre-post-synaptic inhibition Possible increased tendon type III collagen turnover	**Possible** changes in inter- and intra-muscular coordination

Fig. 4.1 Structural versus neural changes.

FUNDAMENTALS OF TRAINING

```
         ┌──────────────────┐
         │   Acceleration   │
         └──────────────────┘
                  ▲
                  │
         ┌──────────────────┐
         │ Countermovement jump │
         └──────────────────┘
                  ▲
                  │
         ┌──────────────────┐
         │    Back squat    │
         └──────────────────┘
```

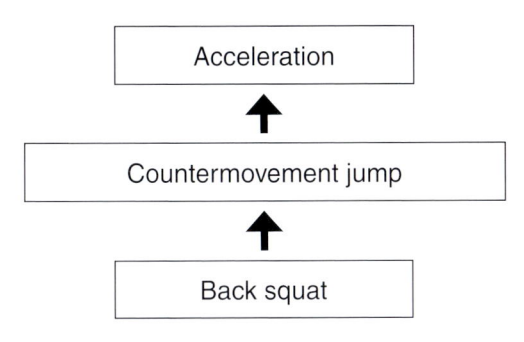

Fig. 4.2 Upward causation training model.

COACHING QUESTIONS

- What specific structural changes need to be made to increase the potential for a positive change in movement?
- What muscles need to do what in the outcome task to create the desired change?

be seen by using the often implicit model in Fig. 4.2.

The mental model in Fig. 4.2 describes a hierarchical pattern to exercises with 'lower order' exercises/tasks affecting the 'higher order' exercises/tasks. For example, back squat positively influences countermovement jump, which positively influences acceleration. This shows the principle of upward causation. While this model makes logical sense on first viewing, the assumptions that it makes with the upward-facing arrows may blind us to the complex nature of the training process.

The reality of training is that upward and downward causation occur. If there is some level of structural and neural similarity between the three tasks described above, then changes at any level will affect both above and below. This means that increased intensity of acceleration training can and will affect countermovement jump performance. This gives a different lens to view much of the research looking at the correlation between these exercises and similar concepts.

It also provides clarity on whether an exercise is allowing the athlete to express their current potential or develop it. To develop, it must either overload structural qualities that are beneficial to the outcome task and/or neural activation specific to the outcome task. With the example above, the countermovement jump could be seen as an exercise where there is a bias towards expressing our current potential, the back squat biased towards changing some structural qualities and acceleration tasks would give athletes the biggest opportunity to change the neural activation specific to the outcome task.

Exercise/Programme Intention

The challenge the previous section presents to coaches is how aligned the exercise or programme intention is with sports performance and the specific methods chosen for the individual. While no programme can be seen as 'right' due to factors described above, the more appropriate outcome is to deliver programmes that are coherent – there is a clear and logical link between the desired change in movement, the programme and/or exercise intention and the method selected. Based on the previous section the key training intentions can be biased towards:

1. **Structural development.** Intention is to change structural qualities that you believe will positively influence the outcome task. (The outcome of this includes changes in structure such as muscle/tendon cross-sectional, pennation angle and so on.) The selection of the training method here is directed by the specific change you hope to make, and can be described as **adaptation-led** and therefore specifics should be coherent with **physiological principles** of adaptation. For example, specific changes in cross-section area may be believed to be required in the hamstrings to positively affect their potential to generate force in high-speed running and cutting tasks.

FUNDAMENTALS OF TRAINING

2. **Coordination development.** Intention is to change coordination believed to positively influence the outcome task. (The outcome of this should be specific changes in movement that can be observed.) The selection of the training method here is directed by the specific changes hoped to be made to the outcome task and can be described as **intention-led** as the intention of this task should match that of the outcome task. The specifics should be coherent with **motor learning principles**. An example of this may include the use of high-load hip dominant/dynamic kettle bell swings to enhance high-speed cutting. From an 'intention' perspective it could be argued that on a 'local' level the intention of the hamstring group is specific to the outcome task in preventing hip flexion and producing hip extension, and if done correctly the muscle/tendon interaction should be specific.

3. **Specific skill emergence.** Intention is to create the conditions 'in context' for positive changes to occur in the outcome task. The conditionings and environment created should be consistent with the outcome task and **context-led**. The specifics should be coherent with **learning principles**. The simplest question here being *'is what the learners are seeing, hearing and feeling similar to the performance environment?'*[18]

Fig. 4.3 aims to assist with the interpretation and application of these concepts by highlighting the key themes, principles and then coaching questions to bring this to life for the coach. It must be stressed that what is being presented is a framework and not a model. While a model can be seen as static and a description of how something is, a framework should be seen as more dynamic and as a tool to assist in exploring beliefs, thinking and possible blind spots. The intention is that this can assist with gaining insight, which will be discussed further below.

The Argument for the Extremes: Rowing

The implicit assumption within the principles and framework described above is that for training to be 'most effective' it must be directed towards developing structure, coordination and sport-specific skills based on the principles described. If the principles 'make sense' and are seen as robust, the most effective training programmes would spend the most directed attention on exercises and sessions that adhered fully to these principles. It must be noted that the wider context should and does allow the inclusion/discussion of areas such as mental rehearsal, team dynamics and wider socio-cultural factors that may influence, help or hinder the training process.

WHAT IS INSIGHT AND HOW IS IT CREATED?

This chapter started with the statement that

> the intention is to provide a framework that more adequately allows practitioners/coaches to explore new and novel ways of looking at training to ensure a more individual specific, performance-focused and insight-generating process [and that for training to be useful it must] produce insight that positively impacts future training.

Both of these statements fit with the view that training is a creative act and so requires the balance between consistency and newness. This newness can be described as insight – an unexpected shift in understanding from one story to another[19] where some initial beliefs are usually abandoned or replaced.

One approach to aiding this in coaching may be to:

FUNDAMENTALS OF TRAINING

		How confident are you that this is word for word what the coach and athlete would say? 0–100%
Performance Intent		
What is the performance goal for the athlete/team?		%
For this to be achieved:		
What needs to change in the data?		%
What would you be able to see the athlete doing in performance that they don't do now?		%
What would the coach/athlete say that they are not seeing now?		%
How will you know you are making progress?		%
Training Intent		
What % of your programme are you confident creates structural change that is specific to the performance goal?		%
What % of your programme are you confident creates changes in movement that is specific to the performance goal?		%
What % of your programme are athletes seeing, hearing and feeling similar to the performance environment?		%
Coaching Intent		
Which coaching behaviours/process do you believe most enhance the change(s) you are trying to make?		%
Which coaching behaviours/process do you believe most hinder the change(s) you are trying to make?		%

Fig. 4.3 Training insights tool.

FUNDAMENTALS OF TRAINING

- Use frameworks to explore our personal beliefs/assumptions.
- Be explicit about our hypothesis and intentions to use as a reference point to reflect/review against.

This approach, if done well, should allow coaches to gain insight in key ways described by Klein:[20]

1. **Contradiction** – you see something is inconsistent.
2. **Connection** – you see patterns/connections you did not see before.
3. **Creative desperation** – you find something is not working and need to think again quickly.

For this reason, this chapter finishes with a tool to support coaches in gaining insight that positively impacts future training decisions (Fig. 4.4). The tool uses many of the principles and concepts described in this chapter and should be supported by the specific content within the forthcoming chapters. The invitation is to complete and review this on a regular basis and use this as an opportunity to share with others, be supported and challenged on your thought process and be persistently curious about creating new and useful solutions.

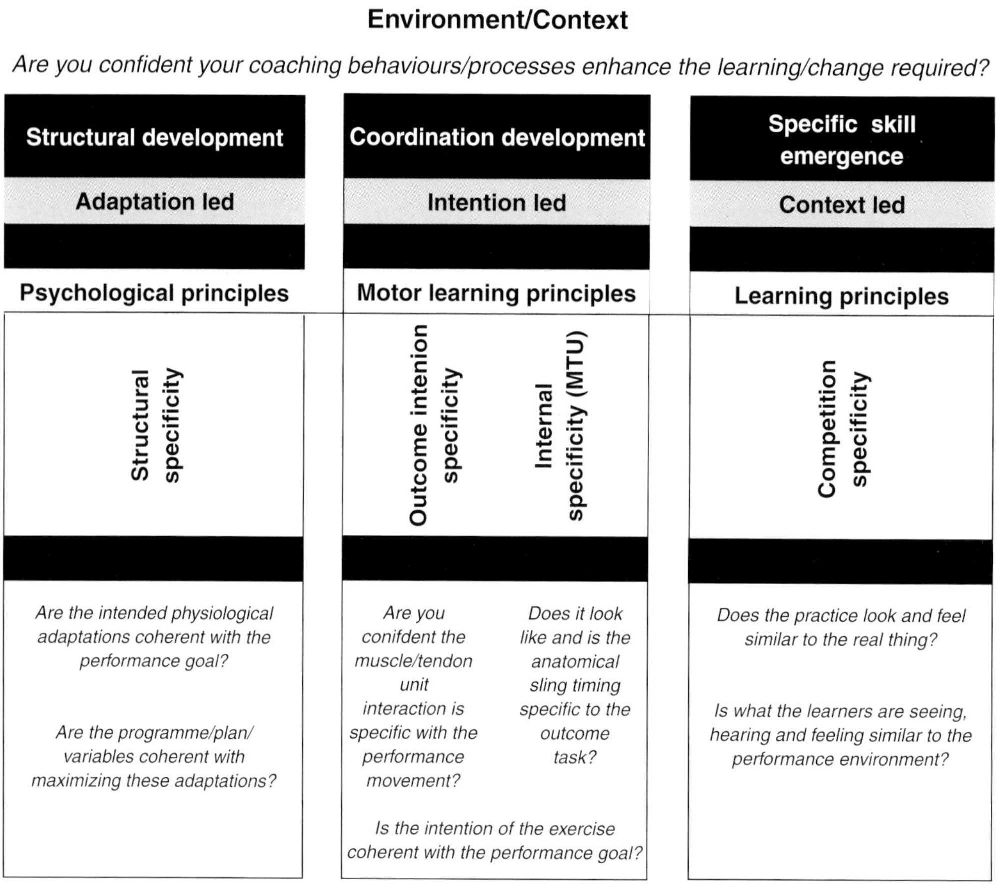

Environment/Context

Are you confident your coaching behaviours/processes enhance the learning/change required?

Structural development	Coordination development	Specific skill emergence
Adaptation led	Intention led	Context led
Psychological principles	**Motor learning principles**	**Learning principles**
Structural specificity	Outcome intention specificity / Internal specificity (MTU)	Competition specificity
Are the intended physiological adaptations coherent with the performance goal? Are the programme/plan/variables coherent with maximizing these adaptations?	Are you confident the muscle/tendon unit interaction is specific with the performance movement? Does it look like and is the anatomical sling timing specific to the outcome task? Is the intention of the exercise coherent with the performance goal?	Does the practice look and feel similar to the real thing? Is what the learners are seeing, hearing and feeling similar to the performance environment?

Fig. 4.4 The training canvas.

REFERENCES

1. Sieden, J. S. (2012). *A Fuller View: Buckminster Fuller's Vision of Hope and Abundance for All*. Colorado, USA: Divine Media Arts.
2. Robins, R., Wheat, Jonathan, Irwin, G., & Bartlett, R. M. (2006). The Effect of Shooting Distance on Movement Variability in Basketball. *Journal of Human Movement Studies*, 50, 217–38.
3. Koenig, G., Tamres, M., & Mann, R. W. (1994). The Biomechanics of the Shoe-Ground Interaction in Golf. In A. J. Cochran, & M. R. Farrally (Eds.), *Science and Golf II* (pp. 40–45). London: E. & F. N, SPON.
4. Dawson, R. G., Lockwood, R. J., Wilson, J. D., & Freeman, G. (1998). The Rowing Cycle: Sources of Variance and Invariance in Ergometer and On-the-Water Performance. *Journal of Motor Behavior*, 30, 33–43.
5. Donoghue, O. A., Harrison, A. J., Coffey, N., & Hayes, K. (2008). Functional Data Analysis of Running Kinematics in Chronic Achilles Tendon Injury. *Medicine & Science in Sports & Exercise*, 40, 1,323–35.
6. Madeleine, P., Mathiassen, S. E., & Arendt-Nielsen, L. (2007). Changes in the Degree of Motor Variability Associated with Experimental and Chronic Neck–Shoulder Pain During a Standardized Repetitive Arm Movement. *Experimental Brain Research*, 185, 689–98.
7. Rathleff, M., Samani, A., Olesen, C., Kersting, U., & Madeleine, P. (2011). Inverse Relationship Between the Complexity of Midfoot Kinematics and Muscle Activation in Patients with Medial Tibial Stress Syndrome. *Journal of Electromyography and Kinesiology*, 21, 638–44.
8. Carson, H. J., Collins, D., & Richards, J. (2013). Intra-Individual Movement Variability During Skill Transitions: A useful marker? *European Journal of Sport Science*, 14, 327–36.
9. Chow, J. Y., Davids, K., Hristovski, R., Araújo, D., & Passos, P. (2011). Nonlinear Pedagogy: Learning design for self-organizing neurobiological systems. *New Ideas in Psychology*, 29, 189–200.
10. Wu, H. G., Miyamoto, Y. R., Castro, L. N., Ölveczky, B. P., & Smith, M. A. (2014). Temporal Structure of Motor Variability is Dynamically Regulated and Predicts Motor Learning Ability. *Nature Neuroscience*, 17, 312–21.
11. Thelen, E., & Fisher, D. M. (1982). Newborn Stepping: An explanation for a 'disappearing' reflex. *Developmental Psychology*, 18, 760–75.
12. Chow et al. (2011).
13. Galea, J. M., Ruge, D., Buijink, A., Bestmann, S., & Rothwell, J. C. (2013). Punishment-Induced Behavioral and Neurophysiological Variability Reveals Dopamine-Dependent Selection of Kinematic Movement Parameters. *Journal of Neuroscience*, 33, 3,981–88.
14. Kelso, J. A. S. (1995). *Dynamic Patterns: The self-organization of brain and behavior*. Cambridge, MA: MIT.
15. Pekny, S. E., Izawa, J., & Shadmehr, R. (2015). Reward-Dependent Modulation of Movement Variability. *Journal of Neuroscience*, 35, 4,015–24.
16. Ranganathan, R., & Newell, K. M. (2013). Changing Up the Routine. *Exercise and Sport Sciences Reviews*, 41, 64–70.
17. Carroll, T. J., Selvanayagam, V. S., Riek, S., & Semmler, J. G. (2011). Neural Adaptations to Strength Training: Moving beyond transcranial magnetic stimulation and reflex studies. *Acta Physiologica*, 202, 119–40.
18. Renshaw, I., Davids, K., Newcombe, D., & Roberts, W. (2019). *The Constraints-Led Approach*. Abingdon, Oxfordshire, UK: Routledge.
19. Klein, G. (2017). *Seeing What Others Don't: The remarkable ways we gain insights*. London, UK: Nicholas Brealey (UK).
20. *Ibid*.

5 | NEUROMUSCULAR PERFORMANCE

Between the idea and the reality, between the motion and the act falls the shadow

T. S. Eliot[1]

INTRODUCTION

As described in the previous chapter, training adaptation can be viewed from a coordinative bias or structural adaptation bias. The following chapters will start to outline the detail around the structural adaptations required for rowing. These have been loosely termed as neuromuscular performance. What will be presented is very similar if not the same as most of the S&C textbooks and articles that cover this area. Details around exercise prescription and assessments will be covered, as will the intended outcome. However, the point of difference is the order in which this information is displayed.

The majority of texts and resources available often describe the methodology of training as the outcome. For example, strength training is a methodology that has multiple outcomes. How the strength training is performed will determine the outcome. This is not specific enough and leads to a large degree of ambiguity between colleagues of what is actually being developed. To take this one step further, the term 'strength' is equally generic. 'Strength' means many things to many people. Having worked with numerous practitioners from multiple disciplines, coaches and athletes, all their definitions and understanding of strength vary. This can create a degree of confusion or as experience shows, more likely frustration. A physiotherapist may use the term 'strength' to define anything where the intensity is above that of low-level motor control activity, whereas the S&C coach is most often referring to something to do with very high-load training. Even among S&C coaches, the definition of 'strength' and 'strength training' varies. By defining the expected change required through the method employed to do this will not provide clarity to the athlete or the team who support them. There have also been occasions where S&C coaches attempt to describe the neuromuscular changes required by the exercise employed to change it. For example, stating the rower needs to improve squat performance is so non-specific, it would be difficult for anyone to truly understand what a successful outcome would be. Squats can be performed with many repetitions with bodyweight through to significant external loading for a very few repetitions. How the squat is performed will determine the neuromuscular adaptation, so stating squat performance needs to improve does not provide this clarity. The more pressing question is what specifically is the squat actually trying to change? Are practitioners and coaches alike able to articulate the intended adaptive response in detail?

On a number of occasions, the terms 'strength', 'strength training' and 'strong' have been banned within the discussion. This forces the conversation to talk specifically about the intended adaptive response. This firstly makes S&C coaches critically think around what the intention of the training programme is. Secondly, it provides a clarity to all involved to explore options around how best to attain the intended outcome. What terms would be used if 'strength', 'strength training' and 'strong' were not available?

INTENDED OUTCOME OF TRAINING

If training is to be described by its outcome and generic terms such as 'strength training' are not specific enough, what is the alternative? Table 5.1 outlines the main training adaptations and how they are best achieved. Each training adaptation is defined

Table 5.1 Training methods based on intended outcome

Outcome	Method	Load	Frequency	Sets	Reps	Temp/Velocity	Testing
Maximal Force Expression	Heavy Strength Training	>80% /MVC	× 2–5/ week	6–10 per body segment	1–8	Explosive to 202	1–3 Repetition max (proxy) Isometric maximal force (F_{max}) Isokinetic maximal force (F_{max})
Rate of Force Development	Explosive Strength Training	Low Load / Medium Load / High Load	× 2–5/ week	6–10 per body segment	1–8	Explosive	CMJ (Impulse characteristics and peak instantaneous power) Isometric rate of force development (RFD) Isokinetic rate of torque development (RTD)
Muscle and Tendon Mass	Hypertrophy	>70% Rep Max /MVC	× 3–6/ week	6–20 per body segment	10–25+	202 to 303	Anthropometrics (body mass, skinfolds and girths) Dual-energy X-ray absorptiometry (DEXA) Magnetic Resonance Imaging (MRI)
Tissue Tolerance	Work Capacity	30–80% Rep Max /MVC	× 3–6/ week	3–10 per body segment	10–25+ or 3–8 mins	101 to 303	Isolated muscle testing to failure (i.e. trunk tests)

by the intended outcome first and the method second. This is an important differentiation as described throughout this chapter. By framing it this way around, the entire support team and the athletes will truly understand what the intention is within the current training method. The table is very specific with the type of strength training terminology being used. Based on this model, if strength training is a method and not an outcome, how relevant is the often-asked question 'How strong is strong enough?' As strength and strong do not define a neuromuscular adaptation, the question is irrelevant. A significantly more relevant question would be 'What are the maximal force requirements of the leg extensors during the drive phase of the rowing stroke?' This question is outcome driven and has a clear relationship to performance over generic first principles of strength training.

The four main outcomes of Table 5.1 are:

1. Maximal force expression.
2. Rate of force development.
3. Muscle and tendon mass.
4. Tissue tolerance/work capacity.

A fifth outcome is muscle-tendon stiffness using plyometrics as the method. However, this is so rarely used (if at all) for rowers that it is not necessary to spend time discussing. The main reason for its exclusion is the vast magnitude of time difference between completing a plyometric-based exercise and the rowing stroke. As discussed in the previous chapter, there is a need for some coordinative similarity between training and competition task. There is little to no coordinative similarity for plyometrics and rowing.

Over the next four chapters, these four outcomes and how they relate to improving rowing performance will be explored. Case studies will be used to bring each area to life, including the decision-making around the programming.

FUNCTION IS A PRODUCT OF OUTCOME

One of the supporting principles that drive these neuromuscular adaptations is to place the rower in the best possible position to optimize training adaptation. This may mean using alternative methods to traditional barbell exercises. While the majority of S&C coaches will have gone through an education of weight room exercise technique, barbell exercises may simply not be the most appropriate exercise to complete. Chapter 11 discusses common injuries in rowing populations. Low back pain, injury and dysfunction are probably the most common. A rower with low back dysfunction will only tolerate a certain amount of spinal loading. In this example a rower with previous low back pain and injury has the training intention to develop maximal force expression of the hip and knee extensors and the back squat has been identified as an exercise to develop this. The limiting factor of maximally loading the hip and knee will be the lumbar spine load tolerance. The rower may never develop the maximal force expression of the hips and knees due to the lumbar spine being unable to tolerate a load great enough to overload the musculature around the hips and knees. If this is the case, what is the rower changing? Probably not much around the hips and knees. Most of the adaptation or maladaptation is likely to be around the spine (Chapter 11 discusses this in more detail).

The exercise and the loading are no longer appropriate for the intended outcome. When the intended outcome is very specific, this provides great flexibility to find alternative methods to develop it. Using the same example, the rower could use a leg press and barbell hip extension using the maximal force expression training guidelines to develop knee and hip maximal force expression respectively. To support the continued development of the spinal loading capability, the rower can also undertake a specific trunk-training programme. By changing the rower's exercises within the principles of maximal force expression, the rower is still able to meet the intended outcome and is likely to reduce the onset of lumbar spine pain and injury with the back squat being removed. There have been examples where the main exercise selection for rowers has been entirely machine-based. The decision-making factor for some of the rowers was that the risk of barbell lifting was too great in terms of potential onset of pain or injury. With a pain- and injury-free rower, most of the entire training programme would be completed. It is the chronic training effect that will ultimately improve a rower's performance.

For a group of female rowers who were embarking on a Pacific Ocean ten-month row, the training experience of the team was low. To make significant changes in preparation for this world record attempt, the decision was made to only include machine weights to develop maximal force and muscle mass. This allowed more time for adaptation and less time required to learn new movements and exercises. While this is not advocating machine weights over barbell exercises, when the intended outcome is the primary goal, the exercise selection becomes secondary to this and therefore does not govern the type of training being completed. As highlighted above, having a very specific outcome provides significant flexibility in the exercise and training methods employed to reach that outcome. S&C coaches often limit the thinking to traditional barbell exercises. Do not be afraid to explore alternatives if that will help the rower meet the intended outcome.

During a recent lecture to postgraduate physiotherapists and doctors, a discussion around 'functional' training started which is worth sharing. One student commented that loading exercises that look like the task may be more functional than traditional strength-training methods, with another student stating barbell exercises are more functional than machine weights. To answer these questions appropriately, the definition of what 'functional' means must be established. Function is the product of the outcome required by an athlete and not that of the methods used. For example, 'functional training' is commonly used to describe barbell exercises or movements which visually look similar to functional human tasks such as squatting, lunging, pushing and pulling to name a few. Describing function in this way is using training methods to describe the outcome with little or no regard to outcome. Describing function as a product of the outcome will state the adaptation or expected change required. An example for a rower would be maximal force expression of the hip and knee extensors. This describes the outcome without reference to a method, allowing the coach to identify any number of methods to achieve this, including barbell or machine weights if required.

To go one step further and attempt to answer the question of movements that visually look similar to the sporting task as being 'functional' and relevant to athletes, the coordinative elements at a cellular level need to be explored further. For two tasks to be coordinatively similar and therefore 'functional', the rate, timing and magnitude of muscle contraction and the contraction type must be near identical (*see* Chapter 4 for more detail). While rowing at a rate of 18–20 strokes per minute may look visually identical to rowing at 40–42 strokes per minute, the rate, timing and magnitude of muscle contractions are entirely different and are therefore coordinatively different tasks with limited crossover. To test this further, jogging and high-speed running look similar, however rate, timing and magnitude of muscle contractions are entirely different. The use of jogging to develop high-speed running is commonly known as an ineffective training method. Yet in the weight room, the use of exercises that visually look like the task athletes compete in has been observed. When the coaches are questioned around the efficacy of the method, often the reply is 'it looks like the task'. This shows a disregard of the adaptive response and the coordinative components that make up every human movement. Function is the product of the outcome and not a methodology to subscribe to.

CLARITY OF OUTCOME

Being very specific with the outcome provides the opportunity to be prognostic in terms of what an S&C coach would expect to change during the programme. When rowers do not achieve the intended outcome, the first place to look is the training programme and the exercise prescription detail. Based on the maximal force expression principles, a rower must lift at near maximal loading for a few repetitions (for example, 1–8 repetitions). Many athletes will do this but show little or no sign of improvement. For some the load is simply not high enough. A simple assessment would be to ask the rower on the last set to complete as many repetitions as possible. If the rower far exceeds the load prescribed, increase the load. If the rower is performing the same or a couple more repetitions, consider the discussion in the previous paragraph.

Using an example of a female athlete from a team sport that a colleague was programming for, a discussion was had around the athlete's maximal force development of the leg extensors. The athlete had made no significant changes in the load lifted over the last 12–16 weeks and additional assessments using force plates concluded the same thing. When looking at the programme, the athlete was on paper prescribed training intensities and repetitions following the principles for maximal force expression. The coach stated the athlete could only lift one more repetition above that prescribed when asked to complete a maximum repetition set.

The coach agreed to the athlete's training session being observed. The athlete was seventeen years old with less than twelve months' training history. The coach had prescribed four sets of five repetitions for back squats. It was only when the athlete started to perform the exercise that it made sense. The athlete was squatting 40kg. While this was the maximum load the athlete could lift, the athlete weighed closer to 65kg. The load was simply not enough to overload the maximal force expression of the leg extensors. The limiting factor to the load was not that of the leg extensors but something else. There are many reasons why the athlete was unable to lift a significantly greater load and the question raised was whether this athlete should be attempting this type of training or not.

However, the simple fact was that while the programming on paper followed the principles, the reality of what was being completed did not. The quote at the start of the chapter by T. S. Eliot is a reminder that what is planned and completed may not match. The principles set out in the following chapters are exactly that. They will not account for how programmes are being completed. The art of coaching is to ensure that the principles are delivered by the rower while training. Observing differences between the intended outcome and the execution, the motivation and understanding by rowers of the intended outcome and creating an environment allowing rowers to execute the plan are just a few examples to consider around this point. The most important point in this and the next four chapters is this: as S&C coaches, the purpose is to train the outcome, not the exercise or method. What needs to occur to make this happen?

REFERENCES

1. Eliot, T. S. (2002). *Collected Poems 1909–62*. London, UK: Faber and Faber Limited.

6 | MAXIMAL FORCE EXPRESSION

Doing something unimportant well doesn't make it important

Tim Ferriss[1]

DEFINING MAXIMAL FORCE EXPRESSION

Strength training is a method to attain a biological adaptation and not the outcome itself. There have been many conversations over the years with fellow S&C coaches, supporting practitioners, coaches and athletes where there is confusion between parties around what we are really trying to change. The problem stems from a lack of clarity; a lack of clarity of the adaptation that is being targeted, a lack of clarity between individuals of the definition of training outcomes (for example, physiotherapists' description of the term 'strength' is often different to that of S&C coaches) and a lack of clarity in defining the intended outcome.

As described in the previous two chapters, clarity of outcome is fundamental to determine biological changes within all *Homo sapiens*. Chapter 5 described four fundamental neuromuscular adaptations that are important for the development of rowers, the first being maximal force expression. This is commonly termed heavy strength training, max strength or something similar to these terms. The reality of these commonly used terms is that they are describing the methodology. These terms do not give any indication of what the S&C coaches' intended outcome is or what it is trying to change, only the methods employed.

Maximal force expression can be defined as just that, the maximum amount of force a single or collective group of muscles can produce.[2] To take this further, this is related to the maximum amount of torque around a joint that can be produced during a specific movement task. The development of maximal force expression must relate back to a given task to be useful to undertake. For example, unpublished data from working with rowers shows the hip and knee are near equal in the contribution of force during the drive phase of the rowing stroke. Developing the concentric maximal force expression of the hip and knee extensors is clearly useful for rowers and provides absolute clarity on what adaptive response coaches are trying to change:

- **Concentric:** muscle contraction type.

- **Maximal force:** ability to increase the force-producing capability of the specified musculature.
- **Hip and knee:** joints which the training programme and adaptive responses are targeted at.

With this explicitness, it becomes clear to all what the intended outcome of the training programme is. This does three things:

1. Provides the coach with the opportunity to explore the most effective methods (training techniques or exercise selection) to attain the proposed outcome.
2. Provides the coach with clarity of how to measure change.
3. Provides the coach with the opportunity to explore the most effective methods (training techniques or exercise selection) to attain the proposed outcome.

As described in Chapter 4, the explicitness does not always need to come from data or research. Experience is equally valid. However, the critical point is whether the plan is logical, does it fit the facts of the athlete and context, and will it have an impact in the real world? Very few of us will have the opportunity to have resources available to collate large volumes of data or research completed on the athletes worked with. The questions posed in Chapter 4 around fitting the facts and whether the plan is coherent and logical will guide coaches to creating explicit outcomes to be generated and programmed and coached with a higher degree of certainty in its effectiveness to meet the intended outcome.

There are two overarching adaptive responses to maximal force development, each with their own multiple adaptive processes. These are:

1. Neural adaptations.
2. Morphological adaptations.

Table 6.1 identifies several neural and morphological adaptations. It is beyond the scope of this book to go into detail around this area, so for brevity, these will be discussed in enough detail to help the decision-making process around effective programming. For those who want a greater depth of understanding, the book *Strength and Conditioning: Biological Principles and Practical Applications*[3] is highly recommended, as is the article by Folland and Williams.[4] The focus of the neuromuscular outcomes in Chapters 7 and 8 are governed by the two overarching adaptive responses identified above but manipulated slightly differently to elicit the desired outcome.

It is important to note the neuromuscular and morphological adaptations outlined in Table 6.1 are not exhaustive. As greater methods to investigate previously little or unknown adaptive processes improve, these will continue to inform coaches of what may be occurring at a cellular level when applying a training methodology. It is important to note that it is near impossible or highly unlikely that

Table 6.1 Neural and morphological adaptations supporting maximal force expression

Neural Adaptations	Morphological Adaptations
↑ Motor unit recruitment	↑ Cross-sectional area
↑ Firing frequency	↑ Pennation angle
↑ Rate coding	↑ Collagen turn-over (muscle & tendon)
↑ Motor unit synchronization	↑ Change in muscle fibre distribution
↑ Inter & intra muscular coordination	

an exercise programme can preferentially bias a single adaptive process in isolation.

A recent discussion with an S&C coach around this topic is worth sharing. Understanding all the known neuromuscular and morphological adaptive processes may be beneficial to recognize for programming but how much will it really alter how programmes are written? The discussion highlighted evidence from a recent research article demonstrating that the measured adaptive response was increased with a specific type of programme prescription. This was evidence enough for the coach to undertake specific training methods to 'preferentially' bias a single adaptive process. However, when pressed about what other programme prescriptions were assessed and how effective they were in positively enhancing that singular adaptive process, the reply was that the study did not investigate any alternative exercise prescriptions. When suggested that other prescriptions could achieve the same, the coach agreed that it is highly possible this was not the only prescription, nor could it be determined to be the most effective. When further questioned around what other adaptive processes were measured and how certain the coach's perception was of the researcher's belief around the adaptive process being preferentially targeted, the coach could not answer the question. To have any certainty of this, every adaptive process would need to be measured against every exercise prescription, which is near impossible. The point of sharing this discussion is to highlight that no single process is responsible for the adaptations targeted and trying to do so is futile.

Having spent the best part of twenty years writing exercise programmes for athletes, reading historical and contemporary research and supervising PhD students studying within this area, one thing has become very apparent. It doesn't matter what the adaptive process is. S&C coaches and researchers can philosophize over what process was responsible for what, but the reality is, if the maximal force expression has increased, the adaptive outcome has been achieved. There has yet to be a coach or athlete that has ever asked 'What adaptive process was responsible for this change?' Referring to Chapter 1, the outcome of any S&C programme in isolation does not matter and never will. It is only relevant when aligned to the performance outcome. When there is alignment around the performance outcome, the methods and hypotheses of how to create change are simply tools to achieve a greater purpose and nothing more.

When the discussion with the same coach continued, the question was asked who the best S&C coaches were in making changes in maximal force expression. There was agreement on several coaches that were trusted to make these changes. Interestingly, none of these coaches would know (or potentially even care!) what adaptive processes were responsible for the maximal force expression development. What these coaches were outstanding at was the creation, understanding and application of principles aligned to maximal force expression. One coach in particular was discussed further, and it was agreed that not only was this coach probably one of the best to truly change maximal force expression of multiple athletes across multiple sports, but the coach's physiological understanding of the changes was far less than the coach within this discussion. The identified coach was also commended for the outstanding inter-personal skills they possessed, which allowed for trusting and supportive relationships with athletes which no doubt has a significant part to play in all the athletes' progression. With this point in mind, the principles behind exercise prescription and relationships with athletes will probably always be more important than the ability to identify and hypothesize the adaptive process involved. That said, it is important to understand the two overarching adaptations to maximal force expression development being neuromuscular and morphological adaptive responses. Morphological changes may result in increases of body mass. This point will be important to consider when preparing lightweight rowers, as significant increases in body mass will affect crew average competition mass and weight making strategies.

RELATIONSHIP TO ROWING PERFORMANCE

The demands of rowing outlined in Chapter 3 highlight the significance of maximal force expression in relation to rowing performance. Key themes to highlight around maximal force expression and rowing performance are:

1. Peak handle forces are recorded at the start, suggesting a large impact during this part of the race.[5]
2. Rowing economy can be improved through maximal force expression.[6]
3. Rowers with greater force expression capabilities tend to have greater anaerobic capabilities and fatigue resistance than those with less force expression capabilities.[7]

Having worked with rowers for several years, the changes observed in rowers and rowing performances after the completion of focused maximal force expression training is marked. It is always difficult to determine just how much impact any strength-training methodology has. Simply stating the rowers' increased weight room scores does not inform coaches of any change in relation to rowing performance. It informs the coach what rowers have completed in the weight room. However, the regular monitoring of rowers' short ergometer performances (discussed further in Chapter 12) during maximal force expression training provides insights into the transfer of training into rowing performances. Improvements in these ergometer performances during maximal force expression training provide greater evidence of meaningful improvements in the weight room being utilized in more rowing-specific tasks. There is evidence that short ergometer performances have a strong relationship to how fast rowers complete 2,000m on an ergometer, both from an empirical evidence[8] and personal experience standpoint. This makes short rowing ergometer tasks not only useful to determine functional changes from maximal force expression training but also give an indication of the potential to row fast 2,000m ergometer performances. This is an important indicator for coaches when considering crews to compete on the water.

ASSESSING CHANGE

Understanding what changes have occurred is an important factor to consider when prescribing training programmes. Firstly, it creates a reference point to start from as to which programmes can be prescribed for progression. Secondly it provides insight into the actual change that has occurred and how successful the programme and coaching has been to elicit the desired change. Without this reference point, there is nothing to anchor training programmes against, it becomes challenging to determine the degree of change and what was responsible for this change (or in some cases, what was responsible for a lack of or no change).

There are many resources that provide guidance on how to assess weight room changes, with the majority being valid and reliable. Below are several methods that can be administered without expensive equipment, which have been useful while assessing rowers' performances.

In Session Monitoring

Regular monitoring of the load the rower has on the bar for each exercise can be a useful assessment to determine the progressive

MAXIMAL FORCE EXPRESSION

change during a training block. For some rowers, determining the correct load required to elicit an adaptive response may be challenging, especially for those with limited strength training history. Often the load will be lower than what is expected of the rower. Another method used is to ask the rower on the final set of an exercise to complete as many repetitions as possible, regardless of what has been prescribed. Continue to allow the rower to lift in a safe and technically competent manner. Termination of this set is at the point at which the rower is unable to lift any more repetitions, or the technical competency is no longer acceptable. If the rower can only lift 2–3 repetitions more than prescribed, the load is most likely to be correct. A very small increase in load may be appropriate. For rowers who can lift 4 or more repetitions above the prescribed, the load is not great enough. Start by adding a small additional load and observe how the rower performs with it. If the number of repetitions completed above the prescribed is significantly more, greater loads may be introduced.

Repetition Maximum

Alternatively, rowers can complete repetition maximum (RM) assessments where the rower will attempt to lift the greatest load for a given number of repetitions. Typically, RM assessments are completed between the 1–3 repetition range. This can be completed within a training session or as a standalone session. Table 6.2 provides a useful tool to determine 1RM based on the number of repetitions lifted during the assessment.[9] For example, if a rower lifted 100kg for 2 repetitions during a bench pull assessment, the load would be multiplied by the coefficient aligned to repetitions lifted. In this case, the coefficient for 2 repetitions is 1.04. The predicted 1RM is 104kg. Since most weights are in 1.25kg increments, this would be rounded up to 105kg. This method is accurate for lower repetitions (1–3 repetitions). However, there is a greater degree of inaccuracy as the number of repetitions assessed increases. It is also worth noting that RM assessment is physically stressful regardless of the number of repetitions completed. While the load of a 1RM is slightly greater than completing a 3RM, the total stress of the 3RM is greater due to the number of repetitions completed. It is advisable to only complete this type of testing periodically within the training programme, with agreement from the rowing coaches of when and how it best sits within the programme. Rowers are advised to complete a thorough warm-up including several sub-maximal lifts close to the starting load for the assessment. Full recovery is required between assessments to give the rower the best opportunity to continue to improve on the previous performance. Assessments are terminated when the rower is unable to lift the desired load for the given repetitions or the technical competency or safety is compromised; rowers should not 'wrestle' the bar while lifting (see 'Technique is as important as the maximal load for maximal force expression' below).

Once a rower has completed the RM assessment, Table 6.3 can be used to prescribe the loads for each exercise. Using the example above where the rower has a predicted 1RM of

Table 6.2 Repetition maximum (RM) coefficients to determine predicted 1RM reproduced[10]

Repetitions	Coefficient
1	1.00
2	1.04
3	1.09
4	1.13
5	1.18
6	1.22
7	1.25
8	1.29
9	1.33
10	1.36

MAXIMAL FORCE EXPRESSION

105kg for a bench press, the exercise prescription is to complete 4 repetitions. The coefficient aligned to the number of repetitions is 0.9. Multiplying 105kg with this coefficient provides the training load of 94.5kg. As identified above, most weight increments are in 1.25kg, so this load would be rounded up to 95kg. As with Table 6.2, there is a degree of increasing inaccuracy as the number of repetitions are completed. Small adjustments may need to be made while observing the rower lifting.

Table 6.3 Prescribing training loads based on 1RM data[11]

Repetitions	Percentage of IRM	Coefficient
1	100%	1
2	95%	0.95
3	93%	0.93
4	90%	0.9
5	87%	0.87
6	85%	0.85
7	82%	0.82
8	80%	0.8
9	77%	0.77
10	75%	0.75

Assessment Considerations

It is important to note that regardless of the assessment used, there is always a degree of variability within the results. No assessment will provide 100 per cent certainty that the change observed is purely down to the training programme. All assessments will be influenced to a degree by other factors (for example emotional state, stress, sleep, residue fatigue and variability in how an assessment was completed, to name a few). When interpreting the results, these factors must be considered to provide greater insight around what is really occurring. Some pilot testing completed using countermovement jumps (CMJ) demonstrates this nicely. Several athletes completed a series of maximal effort CMJ during the day on several consecutive days. If the assessment is used to determine change in a physical characteristic, and the physical characteristic would be fairly stable during the time course of assessment (the athlete would not make significant changes in this quality within a day or over a few days), the expectation would be that the CMJ performance would be very similar regardless of when it was completed. However, this was not the case. There was a high degree of variability across the day and consecutive days in performance measures that were meaningful. Even within the set of CMJ, there was a degree of variability too. This suggests that assessment is prone to influence from external factors as highlighted above. Inferences around the assessment could be very different depending on when the assessment was completed, which will influence how programmes are prescribed. It is also worth noting that field tests are a proxy of what is being assessed. In this case, using the load on the bar to determine change is a proxy of the maximal force expression. The load does not provide force expression figures; only a force plate or transducer can do this. So again, there is a degree of variability within the assessment that needs to be accounted for. Therefore, when calculating assessment data and results, they cannot be looked at or conveyed in absolute certain terms. This is true for all assessments shared through the book.

PROGRAMMING GUIDELINES

Chapter 5 provides an overview in Table 5.1 of the key variables to consider for maximal force expression development. To ensure the adaptive response is stimulated, loading will need to be at or greater than 80 per cent of repetition maximum. For this to be achieved, the number of repetitions prescribed should be

MAXIMAL FORCE EXPRESSION

	Week 1		Week 2		Week 3		Week 4	
	Sets x Reps	% 1RM	Sets x Reps	% 1RM	Sets x Reps	% 1RM	Sets x Reps	% 1RM
Back Squat	3 × 10	75%	4 × 8	80%	4× 8	82%	5 × 6	85%
Leg Press	3 × 10	75%	4 × 8	80%	4 × 8	82%	5 × 6	85%
Bench Press	3 × 10	75%	4 × 8	80%	4 × 8	82%	5 × 6	85%
Seated Row	3 × 10	75%	4 × 8	80%	4 × 8	82%	5 × 6	85%

Fig. 6.1 High repetition, maximal force expression training programme.

within the 1–8 range. A few years ago, a rower, Chris Boddy, was looking to transition from a lightweight to an openweight rower. Chris has agreed to share some of the programmes throughout this and the next few chapters. Chris's story will be shared in more detail in Chapter 8. The examples are real programmes that Chris completed in the transition period to becoming an openweight rower.

High Repetition

As described above, the required repetitions to elicit an adaptive response are between 1–8. High repetition refers to exercises that have repetitions prescribed between 5–8. It is important that the intensity of the load prescribed is close to what a rower can lift for that number of repetitions. (*See* Table 6.3 to accurately prescribe loading.) This type of training is often prescribed at the start of a maximal force expression training block to provide the rower with enough exposure to high loads to prepare for training with a lower number of repetitions and higher intensity of load. By completing this type of training, the rower will be stimulating the required adaptive response but it will also give the rower a degree of tolerance to a repeated maximal load. Experience has shown rowers require a period of time to focus on this type of training to be able to complete the programmes of greater intensity that follow this training block. Fig. 6.1 provides an example of Chris's programme when completing a high-repetition maximal-force training programme. This type of training can last between 2–8 weeks depending on the training block and the block's intended outcome.

Low Repetition

Low-repetition training programme refers to exercises that have repetitions prescribed between 1–5. *See* Table 6.3 to prescribe the required loading to optimize adaptation. This type of training is often used to help rowers 'realize' the maximal force expression by exposing the rower to high loads for small numbers of repetitions. It will often follow a higher repetition of heavy strength training as outlined above. Experience would suggest rowers are only able to tolerate small, concentrated exposures to this type of training where the majority of sessions are designed like this (2–4 sessions a week). This can last from 2–4 weeks. However, it is worth noting that rowers can often tolerate a session of this type of training if completed only once a week. It is often required for rowers to have regular exposure to this type of loading in preparation for the concentrated training block. Jump-

MAXIMAL FORCE EXPRESSION

	Week 5		Week 6		Week 7		Week 8	
	Sets x Reps	% 1RM	Sets x Reps	% 1RM	Sets x Reps	% 1RM	Sets x Reps	% 1RM
Back Squat	5 × 5	87%	6 × 4	90%	6 × 4	90%	5 × 3	93%
Leg Press	5 × 5	87%	6 × 4	90%	6 × 4	90%	5 × 3	93%
Bench Press	5 × 5	87%	6 × 4	90%	6 × 4	90%	5 × 3	93%
Seated Row	5 × 5	87%	6 × 4	90%	6 × 4	90%	5 × 3	93%

Fig. 6.2 Low repetition, maximal force expression training programme.

ing from higher repetition-based loading to lower repetition-based loading without any preparation can be stressful for the rower. It can take many weeks for the rower to become more comfortable with it, by which time the exposure may be removed, reducing the effectiveness of stimulating the required adaptive responses. Fig. 6.2 is an example of what Chris completed when this type of training was prescribed.

It is worth noting that as there are more repetitions within a single set, the number of total sets for that body part reduces. This is an inverse relationship meaning that as the number of repetitions in a single set reduces, the total number of sets increases. This is a rule of thumb and not fixed. For each body part (legs or arms), 6–10 sets are normally completed. If the repetitions are high per set, the set number is closer to 6. If the repetition number is lower per set, the set number is closer to 10. These sets can be completed across several exercises. For example, a rower can complete 4 sets of back squats and 4 sets of leg presses, totalling 8 sets. Maximal force expression training can be completed 2–5 times a week. More experienced lifters can lift closer to 5 times a week, with less experienced individuals lifting 2–3 times a week. The low-repetition heavy-strength training can be the majority if not all the sessions in the week for short periods of time, typically lasting 4–8 weeks. Any more than this becomes too stressful for the rower. Again, more experienced lifters can tolerate longer periods than those who are less experienced.

General Considerations

When planning training, the two questions that need asking are:

1. How much change is required?
2. How long will it take to make these changes?

These questions should frame the basis of planning and programming. A prognostic view needs to be taken to allow for effective planning. This can challenge S&C coaches. The first question is effectively asking what degree of change is acceptable? To be able to answer this question, a thorough understanding of how this neuromuscular quality is related to performance is required, where the rower is currently with regards to this quality, what the rower may need in the future and how this change in the quality will affect other related neuromuscular qualities (such as rate of force development). Adding to this complexity is having an understanding of how much a change in weight room performance will actually affect changes in maximal force expression. Chapter 1 outlines the idea of a performance backward approach, which is critical to determine answers to these performance questions. Aimlessly increasing load on the bar without alignment to the wider performance need will limit performance.

Recognizing the time it takes to make such changes is also necessary. If developing maximal force expression is a priority and a specific degree of change in this is required, knowing the expected timeframe for this change will allow appropriate planning. All athletes respond differently and those from other sports will respond differently to each other. However, there is the opportunity when working with athlete populations to understand how much change can be expected and how long it takes. There have been several experiences, both personally and working with other S&C coaches, where this was not understood enough, and the resulting planning was limiting to the athletes.

For example, a group of rowers were given the winter period (October to December, almost 12 weeks) to make significant changes in maximal force expression. However, the decision was made to spend a significant amount of this time (8 weeks) to increase work capacity and conditioning and slowly expose the rowers to greater intensity of work. This gave the rowers 4 weeks to make the intended changes. The rowers were nowhere near the expected levels. This was due to the lack of understanding of how long it required the rowers to adapt. If repeated (which it was several times), the two changes that could have been applied to give the rowers a better chance of attaining the intended outcome were:

1. Increase the total period of time from 12 weeks to 16–20 weeks, with the first 8 weeks remaining the same and having an additional 4–8 weeks for maximal force expression development.

2. Change how the distribution of the original 12 weeks was used to provide more time within this for maximal force expression development.

The first option is very difficult within rowing as there are so many other competing training priorities. There may be opportunities to stretch this period a little longer. However, the second option, or organizing training differently, is the most likely and pragmatic way to give rowers the opportunity to make significant changes. Exposing rowers to low-repetition high-intensity maximal force expression training early will support the required changes. If a rower is lifting 3–4 times a week, one of those sessions could be this type of training. Maintaining this throughout the period and increasing the number of sessions of this type towards the end will be effective. To make small changes in loading, 3–6 weeks would be an expected timeframe to do this. For larger changes (greater than 15kg), this can take 6–16 weeks. Knowing this timeframe and the required changes will help to determine what is an acceptable level of change and how best to plan for it.

PRINCIPLES

Ray Dalio, the founder and owner of Bridgewater, the most successful hedge fund investment company, wrote a book outlining the principles that he follows in life and in business, aptly named *Principles: Life and Work*.[12] These principles are the basis for decision-making by creating 'mental models' around specific areas within Dalio's life. They are easily recalled (and written down to be recalled upon) and in times of uncertainty or challenging decision-making, the principle becomes the guide to anchor the next action or decision against. Most coaches will spend a lifetime developing and refining principles to guide decision-making in the physical preparation of athletes. This will differ slightly (or a lot!) from coach to coach but serve the same purpose to quickly recall when necessary. Below are some key principles with some explanation that have been developed over the last twenty years. It must be stressed that these principles do evolve as experiences and greater insights become available, so are a fair representation at the time of writing this book!

Fig. 6.3 Loaded hip bridge.

The Actual Load of an Exercise Must be Close to the Maximal Capability of the Intended Musculature

For an exercise to enhance the maximal force expression of a given musculature, that musculature must be placed under enough strain to stimulate the adaptive response. That sounds simple; however, often the reality is what a rower may lift is less than the load required to elicit the required adaptive response. Referring to Chapter 5 with the example of the team sport athlete, the intent is often correct, however what is actually performed falls short of the required loading to enhance the maximal force expression of a given musculature. Rowers are prone to lumbar spine pain and injury, which can limit the ability to perform many tasks including rowing and/or strength-training methods.

For example, a rower needs a concentric extension force around the hip to be circa 2,000 newtons (N) (approximately 200kg) to elicit a maximal force adaptive response, yet the lumbar spine can only tolerate 1,000N (approximately 100kg). The exercise prescribed to create this change is a back squat. The hip will never experience enough force to elicit a maximal force adaptive response, as the lumbar spine is the limiting factor. As long as the lumbar spine is loaded during any exercise with the primary focus on concentric hip extension, there will never be enough force to make the appropriate adaptive response. To overcome this, either the exercise is changed to remove the limiting factor (for example a loaded hip bridge – Fig. 6.3) or significant work is required around the trunk to allow the lumbar spine to tolerate higher forces (*see* Chapter 14). In most cases, both will be required. If rowers can tolerate exercises that allow the required load to elicit the required adaptive response, they can and should be used. This is not implying all rowers need to find alternative exercises that require spinal loading within them.

Use the Most Effective Exercise to Develop the Maximal Force Quality Required

While this principle again seems straightforward and closely linked to the principle above, it has challenged several S&C coaches in discussions around what this really means. Chapter 5 discussed function being a product of outcome required by the rower and not that of the methods used. This specifically refers to the generally accepted idea within S&C that barbell exercises are deemed to be 'functional' as they 'look' like functional movements and machine weights are 'non-functional' as they do not 'look' like functional movements. Based on Chapter 4's point around function related to outcome, what an exercise 'looks' like is a redundant discussion with regards to function. Many S&C coaches are biased towards the use of specific methods, the most notable being barbell exercises, as many education programmes will describe these as the cornerstone of S&C coaches' programmes. (There is a lack of education in defining the clarity of outcome and the decision-making and creativity to identify the best possible solution to meet the performance question rather than fit the method first then link to the performance question.) This bias often inhibits these coaches to use alternative methods, which often include the use of what these coaches would identify as 'non-functional' methods such as machine weights. If a rower requires maximal knee extension concentric force expression, what would be the most effective exercise to prescribe? It would not be a back squat or deadlift; it would most likely be the knee/quad extension machine or maybe the leg press. When the bias is removed and there is clarity around the outcome, all methods can be considered in the decision-making process.

A previous discussion with an S&C coach working within a female team sport shared some interesting data around force expression on the penultimate step into a cutting action. The data suggested those with the greatest maximal force expression of the legs assessed through an isometric mid-thigh pull also had the best cutting performance assessed by a specific agility test for the athlete cohort. For more information on the isometric mid-thigh pull, refer to Kawamori et al.[13] The athletes had several years of strength-training history, but the loads lifted by some were not in line with what would be expected for female team sport athletes. When asked what the coach's plan was to exploit this opportunity, the response was to heavy back squat the athletes. Interestingly, after a prolonged period, the athletes made little to no change in either back squat or cutting performance. The coach was adamant that the athletes had to squat and when questioned what other alternatives could be used to develop the maximal force expression of the legs, the coach was stuck with the idea of squatting and deadlifting – some of the athletes were squatting 50kg for 3–4 repetitions weighing closer to 70kg. This is far from impressive lifting and there may be many reasons for not being able to squat more. However, the coach was caught in the internal bias of barbell exercises are functional – functional being what an exercise looks like and not the outcome needed for the athlete. The coach continued to fail to make any significant or meaningful changes and eventually left the sport without making any impact on that sport. Again, this point is not about barbell exercises versus machine exercises, it is about understanding the intended outcome and having an unbiased view that all exercises can be considered within the decision-making to achieve this outcome.

Rowers Need Regular Exposure to Maximal Force Training Throughout the Season

Rowers can be classed as endurance-biased athletes. While rowers need a degree of maximal force expression, when compared to say, sprinters, rowers are not high-force biased athletes. This means that rowers will rarely produce maximal force expression values as great as true high-force biased athletes. Rowers tend to take a lot longer to develop greater maximal force capabilities and are generally quicker to lose them. This is especially true of lightweight, female and novice strength-trained rowers.

Several strategies have been used to help facilitate maximal force expression and its decline. Rowers will have regular exposure to maximal force expression training. At least once a week during the entire season (except immediately prior to and during championships) rowers will complete maximal force expression training. Previously, for some rowers, the last maximal force expression training

MAXIMAL FORCE EXPRESSION

may be 4–5 weeks before the championships with 2–4 weeks' break post-championships and 4–6 weeks of building back into this type of training at the start of the winter. This could be between 12–15 weeks without this exposure. By the time rowers have this reintroduced, the current capability is somewhat off where it was at the end of the previous season and it can take the rest of the winter to get anywhere close to the standards previously met. Therefore, the introduction of maximal force expression training is completed almost immediately on the return from the break post-championship. This is coupled with introducing maximal force expression training into the programme as late as possible prior to major competitions and to continue through minor competitions. For some rowers, this has resulted in maximal force expression exposures during major championships. The decision to include this was a joint decision between rowers, coaches and S&C coaches for those who felt it was important to continue or those identified as potentially at higher risk of losing these capabilities with its absence, especially where boat classes are fiercely competitive (at that time, lightweight women and men crews).

One other strategy included a maximum of seven days between maximal force expression training exposures. This was based on some previous work by a colleague in athletics who found a decrement in maximal force expression after ten days during competition periods and observations and tracking of rowers' performances.

A final consideration is the maintenance of lean body mass. For some rowers, peaking for competition would inadvertently drop body mass, including lean mass. A reduction in lean mass most probably will result in reduced capability in the ability to produce the same amount of maximal force. Chapter 8 examines hypertrophy training in greater detail.

Technique is as Important as the Maximal Load for Maximal Force Expression

There is always a tendency when programming and coaching for maximal force expression to assume to continually increase the load the

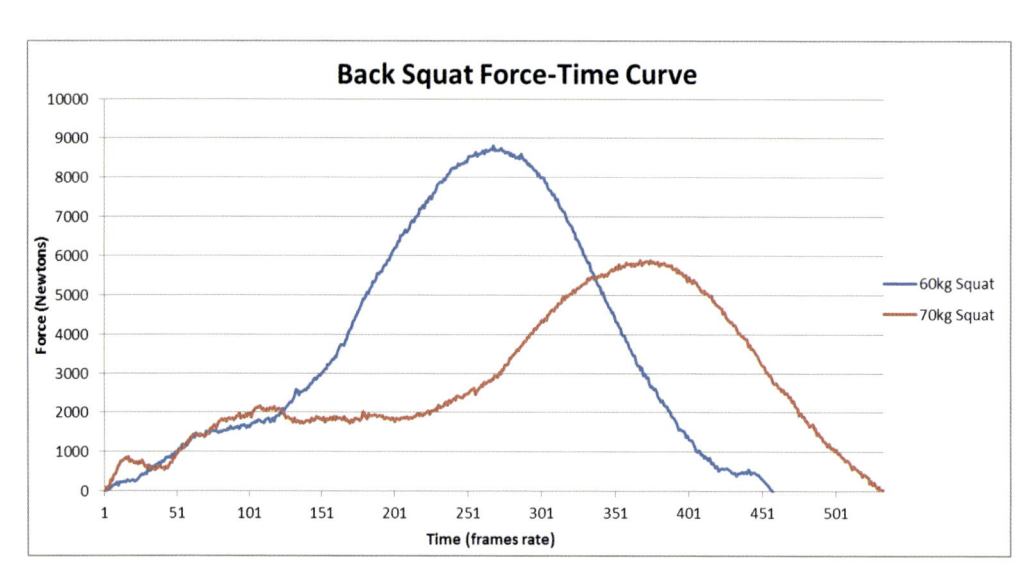

Fig. 6.4 Force-time curve of an individual performing a back squat at two different loads: 60kg (blue) with good technique and 70kg (red) with poor technique.

rower must lift. In principle, this makes sense; to increase maximal force expression, the musculature needs a resistance large enough to stimulate an adaptive response. However there comes a point where an increase in the load a rower is exposed to will cease to be beneficial and may be detrimental.

Fig. 6.4 shows the same individual lifting two different loads on a back squat while standing on a force platform. The force–time curve captures not only the magnitude of force, but the rate of force development. The first force–time curve is of a 60kg back squat (blue line) and the second is the force-time curve of a 70kg back squat (red line). The 60kg back squat was observationally performed with near perfect technique while the 70kg back squat was performed with an observed initial hip lift in the bottom of the descent position before the rest of the trunk and bar started to ascend. (*See* Chapter 13 for more detail and discussion around this particular point as a common fault within rowing populations.)

There are two significant observations of Fig. 6.4. The first is the magnitude of force. The 60kg back squat has an approximately 50 per cent greater magnitude of force compared to the 70kg back squat performance (circa 9,000N and 6,000N respectively). The second is that the rate of force development for the 60kg back squat is significantly more rapid than the 70kg back squat. This demonstrates that good technique as well as sufficient loading is required for maximal force expression, not just load. There have been times when athletes from across multiple sports have been observed 'wrestling' with the bar for an extra 2.5–5kg increase in load believing this is helpful for maximal force expression. It is only helpful if technique does not break down and become the limiting factor.

Adaptive Responses Occur Within a Window of Opportunity

The first international S&C conference was in 2005 in Chicago, USA, where Professor Yuri Verkhoshansky was sharing several keynote presentations. Having devoured pretty much everything available from Verkhoshansky, the conference promised to be truly insightful with the chance to hear many decades of Verkhoshansky's experiences. While it was a fantastic event and lived up to expectations, one of my clearest memories fifteen years on is still not of the content but of the questions being asked of Verkhoshansky. A few of the audience were obsessed with Verkhoshansky giving them the exact sets and repetitions that were thought to be the most optimal for maximal force development. One individual must have asked the same question in a variety of ways at least five times in the hope of finding the magic formula to prescribe to all the athletes that they worked with. At the time there was a feeling of how ridiculous the line of questioning was, as there is no magic set and repetition scheme. Having worked in several roles as an S&C coach over the best part of twenty years, the exposure to S&C coaches who have similar trains of thought has been interesting, to say the least. It is not just the prescription of strength-training methods where this occurs but all areas within S&C, some areas more so than others.

Maximal Aerobic Speed (MAS) is a good example. MAS is the lowest running velocity of an athlete at which the maximum oxygen uptake (VO_2max) occurs.[14] Based on the available assessment of MAS, athletes can be prescribed a training running velocity which is used to help them adapt to greater running velocity at the maximum oxygen uptake. A discussion with a coach around this area sticks out. The coach shared all the running velocities for the athletes. The coach was asked what would happen if the athletes ran 0.1 m/s faster or slower? The very quick reply was that the athletes would not adapt optimally. When pressed further about the certainty of this and the standard error in setting up the training ground for this, the coach became a little more pragmatic. There was acceptance that if athletes did not run at the calculated speed, the athlete would more than likely still adapt if within a range of the intended target. This highlights the key point; there is no magic number to stimulate an appropriate adaptive response. There is a window of opportunity and as long as the prescribed workload is within that window, athletes will adapt.

Observationally and from unpublished data collected, athletes who lift 85 per cent or above of the intended load will continue to longitudinally develop the maximal force expression capability. For example, if a rower is prescribed a deadlift of 120kg but only lifts 110kg, there is a high degree of certainty that the load is still large enough to cause an adaptive response. Based on the 85 per cent principle, the rower could lift as little as 107.5kg and still create an adaptive response. This is useful as it links closely to the principle above around technique but also provides flexibility to the S&C coach in the prescription of training programmes.

Aside note: Verkhoshansky is probably one of the seminal figures within S&C and a vast amount of what is being published or shared today, Verkhoshansky was already doing back in the 1970s and 1980s. His work and thinking is the basis of contemporary S&C – the sixth edition of *Supertraining*[15] is a very worthwhile investment.

Endurance and Neuromuscular Adaptive Responses Can Occur During Concurrent Training

Concurrent training is the simultaneous training of endurance and neuromuscular qualities (such as maximal force expression) within a day or week. There has been a lot of research on concurrent training which has shown the blunting of neuromuscular adaptations from endurance training.[16] However, this has not been experienced within the rowing populations worked with. In fact, quite the opposite.

Analysis of the training data shows on average a 25–30 per cent increase in neuromuscular performances year-on-year. This is a significant increase, which needs a little explaining. As described previously, when comparing rowers to truly high-force athletes, rowers are not comparable in the absolute maximal force expressions. While some maximal force and heavy strength-training performances are impressive, they are impressive across very high-endurance-trained athletes only. Rowers' neuromuscular capabilities tend to start quite low and with limited experiences of truly maximal force expression training (or other neuromuscular qualities development). Improvements can be quite marked when starting from this position. That said, rowers can do approximately thirty to thirty-six hours a week of endurance training, sometimes more. Maximal force expression training may only be two to four sessions a week, which places endurance training at a distinct advantage in terms of opportunity for adaptive responses. Yet rowers continue to develop the neuromuscular qualities year-on-year. Some of the most impressive performances have been observed on training camps at altitude with very high volumes of training (three to four times a day) and rowers continue to produce personal bests on several exercises and assessments. If rowers were to stop all endurance training, neuromuscular performances would have the significant potential to improve further. This however would miss the point that rowers need both endurance and neuromuscular qualities to be successful.

This brings up a very important point. S&C is not the event itself or the outcome, so all planned training must sit within the wider training programme led by the rowing coach. If there is a need for significant changes in maximal force expression, collectively the rowing coach and performance support team need to understand why and how it will fit within the programme. For most rowers, there have been equal positive changes with those who complete neuromuscular training as the first session in the morning to those who have completed it as the last session of the day. With a high degree of certainty, it does not matter what session of the day rowers perform neuromuscular training.

The Intent of Rowers During Training may be the Biggest Contributing Factor to Change

A recent discussion with a group of S&C coaches working with rowers found its way to discuss intent. During the discussion, the delineation of intent and intensity was required, which is worth sharing. Intensity can be defined as the magnitude of workload.

For example, a rower has a predicted repetition maximum of 100kg for the bench pull. When lifting 95kg for 2 repetitions, the intensity is 95 per cent of its maximum whereas lifting 87.5kg for 5 repetitions is 87 per cent of the maximum intensity. In this example, 2 repetitions are at a greater intensity than the 5 repetitions. Intent can be defined as the intended purpose of a rower. It is the directed mental effort applied by a rower within the task. It is applying the right amount of effort for the task and modulating the required intensity for successful task completion, and is related to the attention of rowers during training. Attention can be defined as the ability for rowers to notice and understand the requirements of the task.

Within that recent discussion with coaches, a comment was made that the rowers the coach worked with needed to have greater intensity in the training session. When asked to explain further, the S&C coach identified that the rowers were not lifting enough load on the bar so suggested the intensity of the rowers needed increasing, to help raise the intensity of loading. When asked if rowers stretch their hamstrings with maximal intensity, the S&C coach said no, the rowers would stretch at the required level to get the most out of the exercise. When asked if this is what the S&C coach required while the rowers were lifting in the training session, the coach agreed.

There is a significant difference between intensity and intent yet both are highly connected. What the coach was highlighting is intent: the purposeful actions of the rowers. For rowers to have greater purpose or intent, they first must know what is expected. The rowers need clarity, which must be provided by the S&C coach. Therefore, intention and attention are so closely linked. If rowers are expected to perform tasks in a specific way, the coach must provide the purpose of the training and the required intent to perform this to create the optimal adaptive response. The rower must also recognize how to complete the task effectively and continually self-regulate to ensure they are doing what is required. Again, providing this is the role of the S&C coach. When learning to drive, the driving instructor facilitates the learner to pay attention to the cues in the car, on the road and with other vehicles to safely navigate the journey. This is no different for rowers. The S&C coach must facilitate the rowers to pay attention to the cues within the exercise or session to support the optimal adaptive response. This can mean different things for different types of training. For example, for maximal force expression training, providing expectations of what types of loading are required may change the rower's own expectations of what is good. This can be easily done by providing expected standards and individual targets for rowers. For another type of training such as developing mobility around the hip and thoracic spine, providing rowers with the positions, movements and how it may 'feel' can help rowers apply the correct intent through their attention to the task.

MAXIMAL FORCE EXPRESSION

The Adductor Magnus not the Gluteus Maximus is the Prime Hip Extensor in Deep Flexion

The rowing stroke involves the hip going into deep flexion at the catch (Fig. 6.5). Rowing coaches may also use coaching phrases such as 'engaging the glutes' during the drive phase or the glutes and trunk moving together from the catch to mid-drive phase (around maximal handle force) (Fig. 6.6). This may create some confusion around the actual role of the hip musculature during the rowing stroke, specifically the gluteus maximus (the very large muscles of the buttocks). The coaching terminology of the drive phase being led by the glutes is used to inform rowers not to extend the trunk (increasing the angle of the trunk in relation to the hip) too early, allowing the legs to contribute to the stroke for longer (a long front-loaded leg-drive stroke). If the trunk starts to extend early, the legs' contribution to the rowing strokes becomes reduced with an increased contribution from the trunk. The legs are anatomically more advantaged to produce force during the rowing stroke with the correct rowing technique.

In a lot of textbooks, the gluteus maximus is named as the primary hip extensor. This is correct when the hip is above 90 degrees of flexion (Fig. 6.7). When the hip angle is below 90 degrees (Fig. 6.5), the gluteus maximus ceases to be a prime hip extensor. When observing the musculature around the posterior hip (gluteus maximus) of rowers and sprinters, there are significant differences between the respective masses. Sprinters have large posterior hip mass as sprinting requires very large hip extension forces from 90 degrees of hip extension through to terminal hip extension. Rowers will never fully extend the hip and may only go through 50–90 degrees of hip extension during the rowing stroke, most of the extension occurring from a deep-flexed position. Rowers' posterior hip mass is small in comparison to the sprinters. There simply isn't enough mass to indicate the gluteus maximus as a prime hip extensor. From an adaptive response point of view, if the gluteus maximus were required as the prime hip extensor, the resultant change would be an increase in posterior hip mass. If the gluteus maximus is not the prime

Fig. 6.5 Catch of rowing stroke. Deep hip flexion (below 90 degrees).

MAXIMAL FORCE EXPRESSION

Fig. 6.6 Mid-drive phase/maximal handle force.

Fig. 6.7 Extraction at end of drive phase. Shallow hip flexion (above 90 degrees).

hip extensor from a deep flexion position, what is?

The answer here is the adductor group, specifically the adductor magnus. The adductor magnus is found on the inner thigh and is the only muscle that has the mechanical advantage of extending the hip within a deep flexion position. While there is no empirical evidence of this within the rowing population, the functional anatomy of the hip[17] makes it possible to draw inference to this hip extension mechanism. This brings up an interesting discussion around exercise selection for rowers. How can the adductor magnus be trained as a hip extensor in deep flexion? Firstly, the adductor magnus requires enough mass to be able to do this role effectively, so traditional adductor-based exercises using the principles in Chapter 8 may be useful. Secondly, if exercises place rowers in deep flexion positions such as back squat, leg press or hip bridges, the adductor magnus will be the prime hip extensor and will be able to adapt accordingly. Due to the instability of rowing on water, the adductor muscle group may also be required in maintaining a stable position within the boat. Neuromuscular training of the adductor muscle group is good as not only will it provide the ability to produce maximal force in deep hip flexion, but may also support the rower's stability in the boat.

Single Limb Training Must be Greater than 70 per cent of the Bilateral Equivalent to Develop Maximal Force Expression

There are times when rowers are unable to complete bilateral training exercises, such as the back squat or bench press. Range of movement may be limited or other factors may be in play reducing the loading of the intended musculature. There have been discussions with S&C coaches around whether the use of single limb training can be used to overcome the limitations of bilateral exercises that some rowers may experience. The answer is both yes and no; yes, if the rower can lift greater than 70 per cent of the bilateral equivalent or no if they are unable to.

When working with track and field athletes, the use of isometric mid-thigh pull assessment[18] provided insights around the maximal force expression of unilateral and bilateral leg capabilities. The use was originally intended to monitor bilateral differences to determine any potential injury or performance risk. The unintended consequence was that it also provided knowledge of how much force a single limb could produce in comparison to the bilateral equivalent. Those athletes that were uninjured were able to produce approximately 70 per cent of the maximal force on a single leg that could be produced on two legs. This has been repeated across several athlete populations with similar results. Pilot work had been completed on upper body isometric force measurements that suggested a similar pattern. This provides a good basis for S&C coaches to prescribe appropriate loading for maximal force expression with a higher degree of certainty that the loading will produce an appropriate adaptive response. It is also worth noting that if the reasoning for including single limb training was due to the rower being unable to load heavy enough on the bilateral equivalent to elicit maximal force adaptations, then using single limb loads equal to 50 per cent of the bilateral equivalent will result in the same outcome; the load is simply not heavy enough to stimulate the required adaptive response.

The Limiting Factors While Lifting Should be the Physical Capability and not the Lack of Equipment

A few years ago, while coaching a javelin thrower, a conversation was had with a far more experienced throws coach. While much of the conversation focused around the technical model of throwing a javelin, there was one discussion point around S&C. The coach was adamant that throwers should not use lifting straps while weightlifting. The argument was that throwers need a high degree of 'grip strength' (the force required to adequately hold a javelin and for the grip not to be a limiting factor while throwing) so while lifting from the floor (for example a deadlift) or from hang position (for example a hang clean), the thrower should use grip strength alone to handle the load. At the time it did not sit right but I was unable to articulate what it was that felt wrong. It was only after the meeting that a logical argument was formed to justify the use of lifting straps.

MAXIMAL FORCE EXPRESSION

There is agreement that there is a need for a degree of 'grip strength'. Whilst throwing a javelin, the loads lifted by these high-force athletes were very large. Therefore, during low sub-maximal loading, the force qualities required would be developed enough to support performance. This, however, was not the main concern. The ability to lift loads to develop maximal force expression or rate of force development will be limited by the weakest link in the chain. This is often the athlete's ability to grip the bar effectively. If the ability to grip the bar becomes the limiting factor to lifting heavy enough loads to develop force characteristics of, say, the legs, then the legs will not have a high enough exposure for the required adaptive responses to make the necessary changes. The training becomes limited and the repetitions become wasteful.

However, the use of lifting straps within this example would ensure the athlete is not limited by the grip and therefore is able to stimulate the required adaptive responses to develop force characteristics. Bringing this back to rowers, the way rowers grip the oar is often how rowers grip the weight bar; an open grip (thumb not wrapped around the bar) and bar hanging in the fingertips. This may be adequate for rowing a boat but is certainly not adequate to effectively lift heavy loads. Observing one of the lightweight male rowers' power clean, he was unable to hold on to the bar once it got to hip height and the load became close to maximal. It took a while to diagnose but became obvious the issue was that the rower was gripping the bar like an oar. When lifting straps were introduced, grip no longer became an issue and the rower was able to supersede existing personal bests while also significantly improving technique. The rower was focusing so much on gripping the bar, the rest of the lift became less effective.

This principle should be extended further to:

1. Wearing weightlifting shoes for squatting and Olympic lifting.
2. Removing trainers or lifting shoes when deadlifting.
3. Wearing wrist straps to support the wrist during bench press and pull exercises.
4. Using chalk to assist gripping the bar.
5. Using trap bars for deadlifting if it makes lifting from the floor more comfortable.
6. Using safety squat bars for back squatting if it makes squatting more comfortable.

Rowers with Low Strength-Training History Will Adapt to Any Stimulus. This is not True for Experienced Strength-Training Rowers

Those who have little strength-training history can make quite significant changes with neuromuscular qualities regardless of the type and method of training. For instance, circuit training is a common method of strength training completed within rowing clubs across the world. Those who have little experience of strength training will benefit in changes in neuromuscular qualities after a period of completing circuit training. This may lead to some rowers and rowing coaches believing that circuit training is an effective method to develop neuromuscular performance. The potential reason for rowers improving with circuit training is that the loading is above that of current habitual load, this being the load the rower is currently exposed to and circuit training will provide loading slightly above this. Once a rower becomes more experienced or has a consistent bout of regularly completing circuit training, the rower's habitual load has increased, yet the loading from circuit training has not significantly changed. This is in part due to the nature of how circuit training is completed. The primary adaptive response of circuit training is more work capacity (Chapter 9) or aerobic in nature and not to stimulate neuromuscular changes, therefore it requires a high volume of repetitions or bouts of time. Significantly higher loads cannot be introduced as it would not allow the rower to complete the number of repetitions or complete the time period prescribed. Circuit training is not and will never be a method to stimulate neuromuscular changes unless the principles outlined in Chapter 5 are adhered to.

Once rowers are more accustomed to low-level loading, which becomes the rower's new habitual load, significant changes are required to the rower's training programme to elicit neuromuscular adaptive responses. Without these changes, rowers will cease to continue to adapt or at the very least will only create work capacity adaptive responses. This is not a negative if this is the primary outcome. It is a negative when a neuromuscular quality is the primary adaptive response. There have been several conversations with rowers and rowing coaches around this topic and the evidence provided to suggest low-level loading is an effective method for neuromuscular adaptation for young and novice rowers, but is unable to demonstrate its effectiveness with more experienced rowers. Not a single experienced strength-trained rower worked with has continued to adapt using low-load methods. This makes circuit training redundant when attempting to maximize neuromuscular adaptive responses.

CONCLUSION

This chapter has outlined the key principles and considerations for the development of maximal force expression. Manipulating the training programme to create the desired outcome is a blend of understanding the loading parameters, the principles which ensure the loading parameters are actually being completed and the rowers understanding what is expected of them and how the S&C coach can create an optimal training environment for them to accomplish the desired outcome.

There are no single optimal sets and repetitions for the desired outcome; it is the critical thinking and decision-making of S&C coaches who programme and coach for the continuously evolving rowers. Writing this book has provided the opportunity to refine the principles shared within this chapter. The principles did not naturally sit within a single chapter or section of a chapter, but felt like they would be useful to share. While many of the principles sit within this chapter, some fitted better within the following chapters.

REFERENCES

1. Ferriss, T. (2011). *The 4–Hour Work Week: Escape the 9–5, Live Anywhere and Join the New Rich.* Chatham, UK: Random House.
2. Stone, M. H., Sands, W. A., Carlock, J., Callan, S., Dickie, D., Daigle, K., Cotton, J., Smith, S. L., & Hartman, H. (2004). The Importance of Isometric Maximum Strength and Peak Rate-of-Force Development in Sprint Cycling. *Journal of Strength and Conditioning Research.* 18, 878–84.
3. Cardinale, M., Newton, R. U., & Nosaka, K. (2010). *Strength and Conditioning: Biological Principles to Practical Application.* Oxford, UK: Wiley-Blackwell.
4. Folland, J. P., & Williams, A. G. (2007). The Adaptations to Strength Training: Morphological and neurological contributions to increased strength. *Sports Medicine.* 37, 145–68.
5. Hartman, U., Mader, A., Wasser, K., & Klauer, I. (1993). Peak Force, Velocity, and Power During Five and Ten Maximal Rowing Ergometer Strokes by World Class Female and Male Rowers. *International Journal of Sports Medicine.* 14 (Suppl. 1), S42–S45.
6. Bourdin, M., Messonnier, L., Hager, J. P., & Lacour, J. R. (2004). Peak Power Output Predicts Rowing Ergometer Perform-

ance in Elite Male Rowers. *International Journal of Sports Medicine*. 25, 368–73.
7. Stone, M. H., Stone, M. E., Sands, W., Pierce, K. C., Newton, R. U., Haff, G. G., & Carlock, J. (2006). Maximum Strength and Strength Training – A relationship to endurance? *Strength and Conditioning Journal*. 28, 44–53.
8. Ingham, S. A., Whyte, G. P., Jones, K., & Nevill, A. M. (2002). Determinants of 2000m Rowing Ergometer Performance in Elite Rowers. *European Journal of Applied Physiology*. 88, 243–46.
9. Thompson, P., & Wolf, A. (2015). *Training for the Complete Rower: A guide to improving your performance*. Wiltshire, UK: The Crowood Press.
10. Ibid.
11. Ibid.
12. Dalio, R. (2017). *Principles: Life & Work*. New York City, New York USA: Simon and Schuster.
13. Kawamori, N., Rossi, S. J., Justice, B. D., Haff, E. E., Pistilli, E. E., O'Bryant, H. S., Stone, M. H., & Haff, G. G. (2006). Peak Force and Rate of Force Development During Isometric and Dynamic Mid-thigh Clean Pulls Performed at Various Intensities. *Journal of Strength and Conditioning Research*. 20, 483–91.
14. Billat, V., & Koralsztein, J. P. (1996). Significance of the Velocity at O2max and Time to Exhaustion at this Velocity. *Sports Medicine*. 22, 90–108.
15. Verkhoshansky, Y. C., & Siff, M. C. (2009). *Supertraining*. Super-training Institute, Denver, Colorado, USA.
16. Nader, G. A. (2006). Concurrent Strength and Endurance Training: From molecule to man. *Medicine and Science in Sport and Exercise*. 38, 1,965–70.
17. Kapandji, I. A. (2007). *The Physiology of Joints – Volume 3: The Spinal Column, Pelvic Girdle and Head*. Pencaitland, Scotland, UK: Handspring Publishing.
18. Kawamori *et al.* (2006).

7 | RATE OF FORCE OF DEVELOPMENT

Any fool can know. The point is to understand

Albert Einstein[1]

DEFINING RATE OF FORCE DEVELOPMENT

Rate of force development (RFD) can be defined as the ability to produce the greatest magnitude of force in a given time period.[2] Unlike maximal force expression, with its intention to produce the largest magnitude of force, RFD has the added constraint of time. Under a time constraint, the magnitude of force is likely to be less than that of a task without this constraint. This makes it distinctly unique from maximal force expression and requires potentially different training methods. These methods are typically described as explosive strength training. The intention of this type of training is often to accelerate a body segment or an external load as quickly as possible. For example, jumping on a box would accelerate the body as quickly as possible while throwing a medicine ball would be accelerating an external load.

Unlike heavy-strength training using heavy loading used to develop maximal force expression, explosive strength training to develop RFD can be competed across many modalities from bodyweight, low loads such as using medicine balls and moderate to high loads (jump squats and power cleans respectively). Explosive strength training can therefore include methods which are more velocity biased (bodyweight or low loads) or more load biased (moderate to high loads). Both are effective in changing RFD qualities. However, for rowers with younger training experiences or lumbar spine injury risk, the velocity-biased based training seems to be more effective and less taxing on the lumbar spine.

What's Wrong with Power?

Explosive strength-training methods are often referred to as 'power training' and the outcome as 'becoming more powerful'. This is inherently misleading. In the strictest sense, power is external mechanical output measuring the rate of work.[3] It is not a physical quality, nor does it accurately describe the outcome or method of training well enough to provide clarity to staff or athletes. An extract from the Knudson article articulates why power is an incorrect term and should not be used to describe outcome or method:

RATE OF FORCE OF DEVELOPMENT

The mechanical definition of power is the rate of doing work. Because forces only do mechanical work when movement is present, mechanical power flow is present in most human movements. It is therefore nearly useless to refer to 'power events' or 'power athletes' because all movements except for stabilized postures created by isometric muscle actions, involve muscular power flow.[4]

Every movement a human is involved in has a mechanical power flow; therefore power training is a redundant term. The confusion of its use may stem from the specific form of weightlifting termed powerlifting, where competitors compete in lifting the greatest loads in bench press, back squat and deadlift. The extract above refers to forces completing work that connects more effectively to the correct terminology of RFD.

While it is accepted the term 'power' is probably used to describe the explosive nature of a movement task, the consistency of terminology is required to provide clarity for all individuals involved. Therefore, 'power' is not used to describe the outcome of the method of strength training. Power is referred to consistently in the literature with regards to rowing performance. This has been interpreted as a measure of RFD in the boat or ergometer and inferences made between RFD and rowing performance.

RELATIONSHIP TO ROWING PERFORMANCE

Chapter 3 identifies the importance of rate of force development during racing and for the rowing stroke. The key themes to consider are:

1. Peak rowing ergometer power is a strong predictor of 2,000m performance.[5,6]
2. The largest contribution of force within the rowing stroke is during the drive phase which is time (stroke rate) and distance (length of stroke) constrained.[7]

There is a need to support the rower's ability to produce high mechanical peak powers during the rowing stroke, as the evidence suggests this to be advantageous to 2,000m performances.[8] With the rowing stroke constrained by the amount of time and distance, the rower must produce force (maximal handle force occurs around halfway during the rowing stroke, roughly 0.5 seconds from catch to maximal handle force), RFD training becomes an essential component of the training programme.

It is also worth noting that the movement of drive phase is primarily through concentric muscle contractions.[9] The ratio between the oar being in the water (drive phase) and out of the water (recovery phase) is around 1:3 during low-rating endurance training and closer to 1:1 during competition racing.[10] If a competitive rowing stroke takes around 2 seconds, this would equate to about 1 second for the drive phase and 1 second for the recovery phase. There have been discussions around the use of plyometric-biased tasks to enhance the force production during the drive phase. Plyometric tasks are those that require an eccentric pre-stretch of the musculature and tendons followed by an amortization phase and the concentric muscle contraction. The amortization phase is the period of time between the pre-stretch and the concentric muscle contraction. The benefit of plyometric tasks and their transfer to sporting activities is the utilization of stored elastic energy from the soft tissue. The stored elastic energy is primed during the pre-stretch and if the amortization phase is rapid enough (normally less than 250ms), the energy will contribute to force production alongside concentric muscle contraction. The stored elastic energy does not have an energy cost, unlike muscle contractions, which makes its utilization advantageous. If the amortization phase is longer than 250ms, the contribution of stored elastic energy is lost as heat and will not contribute to force production.

Due to the amount of time during the recovery phase (approximately one second), the rowing stroke is not 'plyometric' in nature. The timeframe is approximately four times longer than the limit of the amortization phase for stored elastic energy to be utilized. Secondly, the recovery phase may not adequately pre-stretch the musculature of the legs to allow the physiological mechanisms to be utilized. The completion of plyometric-biased tasks would be futile to improve a rower's performance, as the muscle contraction timings are entirely different. Concentric-biased exercise selection will be significantly more effective. The reason for sharing this is that often within RFD training, the discussion leads to explore methods that may support the rower's performance with plyometrics suggested as a method due to its explosive nature. Time is best spent elsewhere to develop RFD.

ASSESSING CHANGE

As described in Chapter 6, assessing change is an important component to consider when planning and programming. Whereas changes in maximal force expression can be tracked through the proxy of increasing loads, RFD is a little more challenging. The speed of movement or mechanical output measures (such as mechanical power) are better proxy assessments of change. Below are examples of how assessing change can be achieved.

Within Session Monitoring

With the velocity of the movement being more important to track than the load, the ability to measure velocity of major lifts is very useful. This allows rowers to work at pre-scribed velocities and changes are only made to loads if rowers are able to maintain the prescribed velocity. It also provides rowers a focus away from the load and directly on the intended outcome. This type of augmented feedback allows the rower to provide the required intent to complete the tasks being prescribed.

There are several technologies that are available to track barbell exercises. However, there are a few trade-offs to consider:

1. Cost.
2. Accuracy.
3. Ease of use.

All three of these will play into what system to use. Technology has improved in this area since first attempting to regularly monitor velocity and external power fifteen years ago and will continue to do so, making it easier and cheaper to find a suitable solution at a reasonable price. The use of Gymaware and Tendo has been very useful, especially if only looking to track peak velocity. Gymaware provides a greater degree of accuracy on measuring acceleration. Both are simple to set up using potentiometers (attaching a cord to the bar and displacement of the cord is measured) and provide a visual display for rowers and coaches to inform training intent and outcome. These however may be cost prohibitive for those on tight budgets. The increase in inertial measurement units (IMU) has increased using similar technology in smart phones to determine velocity, acceleration and displacement. These units can be attached to the bar itself or the rower. These are lower cost and easy to use. The reliability of these units has been demonstrated to be more accurate and repeatable which may make them useful devices to use.

Jump Assessment

Using force plates or contact mats, the magnitude of external mechanical peak power can be established through countermovement

RATE OF FORCE OF DEVELOPMENT

jumping (CMJ). Jumping and the measurement of external mechanical peak power has been found to be a good marker of changes in RFD[11] so is a valid and reliable measure of change. This has been a useful tool with the rowers worked with to assess change and inform programming decisions. With many different systems of force plates and contact mats available, all with different methods of collating the data and calculating the output, it is impossible to provide normative or standards of data. This can, however, be easily established with the technology available, making it very specific to the rowing population it is used with. Since this CMJ is a valid and reliable measure, it will provide consistent insights about the rowing population.

This type of assessment tends to be low stress for the rowers, so can be completed fairly regularly. However, its use tends to be at the start and end of training blocks. It is important to note that jumping is a skill. If rowers are not accustomed to jumping, the simple act of jumping will significantly improve the rower's technique and therefore the outcome of the assessment. This may not be as a result of the training prescribed but becoming more familiarized with the assessment. To avoid this, it is recommended that rowers are exposed to jumping tasks similar to the assessment within the training programme. Rowers are also required to warm up prior to assessment, which includes several sub-maximal jumps to give them the best opportunity to perform. Give rowers 3–5 minutes to recover between the final warm-up jump and first assessment jump.

CMJ assessments are highly sensitive to fatigue, so care must be taken when considering when best to complete the assessment. *See* Chapter 6 for a wider discussion on this topic. The use of bilateral force plates such as ForceDecks also provides the opportunity to look at left and right leg imbalances. This can help to restore rowers to a normative balance and help in the rower's return from injury by having benchmarks of previous performances on a single limb. If the availability of technology is limited, using standing broad jumps is also a valid and reliable measure of RFD, which can be effectively used. This assessment is equally suspectable to familiarization. Ensure rowers have the opportunity to practise this jump within training prior to assessment.

Ergometer Assessment

Most boat houses will have rowing ergometers which are also valid and reliable tools to assess change in RFD. The completion of power strokes or short distance sprints will provide the rower and S&C coach with an idea of changes in RFD in a very specific way which is probably more closely related to on-water performance. Chapter 12 provides full details of how best to set up ergometer power strokes. Similar to the jump assessments, the type of ergometer and how the values are calculated vary so it's not possible to share generic normative standards or benchmarks. However, as with the jump assessments, these can be easily established using the protocols in Chapter 12 to ensure reliability and repeatability of the assessment across the rowing population.

PROGRAMMING GUIDELINES

Below are examples of training programmes where the intended outcome is to develop RFD using explosive strength training. The programmes are from the same rower, Chris, who was discussed in Chapter 6, as a lightweight rower attempting to compete in the openweight category.

Explosive Strength Training

Table 7.1 highlights a training programme

and heavy strength-training programming, there is no single solution or exercise prescription that will cover all rowers' needs. The principles of performance backwards and understanding the needs of the rower against the demands of the sport will provide clarity around the programming needs. Optimal thinking over optimal solutions is required. Optimal thinking is being able to recognize the need, the constraints and then the opportunities that exist to create the required change. An optimal solutions approach is producing the same content, regardless of need or constraints. This is limiting through the lack of consideration of the individual and the event. The beauty of being explicit around intended outcome is that it provides freedom to explore all opportunities that may exist to create the change.

REFERENCES

1. Simmons, G. F. (2003). *Precalculus Mathematics in a Nutshell: Geometry, Algebra, Trigonometry.* Arkansas, USA: Resource Publications.
2. Cormie, P., McGuigan, M., & Newton, R. (2011). Developing Maximal Neuromuscular Power. *Sports Medicine.* 41, 17–38.
3. Knudson, D. V. (2009). Correcting the Use of the Term 'Power' in the Strength and Conditioning Literature. *Journal of Strength and Conditioning Research.* 23, 1,902–08.
4. *Ibid.*
5. Bourdin, M., Messonnier, L., Hager, J. P., & Lacour, J. R. (2004). Peak Power Output Predicts Rowing Ergometer Performance in Elite Male Rowers. *International Journal of Sports Medicine.* 25, 368–73.
6. Ingham, S. A., Whyte, G. P., Jones, K., & Nevill, A. M. (2002). Determinants of 2000m Rowing Ergometer Performance in Elite Rowers. *European Journal of Applied Physiology.* 88, 243–46.
7. Thompson, P., & Wolf, A. (2015). *Training for the Complete Rower: A guide to improving your performance.* Wiltshire, UK: The Crowood Press.
8. Bourdin *et al.* (2004).
9. Thompson & Wolf (2015).
10. *Ibid.*
11. Cormie *et al.* (2011).

8 | MUSCLE AND TENDON MASS

We cannot become what we want to be by remaining what we are

Max De Pree[1]

DEFINING MUSCLE AND TENDON MASS

Muscle and tendon mass can be described as a process of increasing the amount of lean muscle and tendon mass. This is typically called hypertrophy training, which uses strength-training methods to achieve the intended outcome. The primary adaptive responses are morphological in nature with increases in muscle and tendon fibres. Deliberate attempts to make significant changes in muscle and tendon mass are separate and quite different to the generic phases often spoken about within S&C texts.[2] Traditional models of performance planning would include generic blocks of training early in the pre-season in preparation to withstand the rigours of subsequent training blocks, which is often termed hypertrophy.[3] The primary focus is less about significant changes in muscle and/or tendon mass and more to do with the ability to increase tolerance to training which may result in small increases in mass. This increase in training tolerance is better described as work capacity, which will be fully explored in Chapter 9. It is a separate but equally important neuromuscular quality to the others shared within this book. However, it should not be confused with muscle and tendon mass development through hypertrophy training, which is why there is an entire chapter dedicated to it.

It is important to address muscle and tendon mass as a separate intended outcome as some – but not all – rowers will require targeted approaches to increase muscle mass through hypertrophy training. When there is this specific need, deliberate planning and programming is required to make these significant changes. Having a general understanding of the mechanisms that may stimulate the adaptive responses will help with this deliberate planning.

Increase in Muscle Mass Mechanisms

An article by Schoenfeld provides an excellent overview of the three mechanisms that need to be stimulated to make changes in muscle mass[4]. These mechanisms are:

1. **Mechanical tension:** muscles must be placed under enough tension to stimulate increases in muscle mass. Loading at the near maximal capability for the number of prescribed repetitions is required (see Table 6.3 in Chapter 6). If loading is not near maximal, the mechanical tension will not be enough to stimulate an adaptive response.
2. **Muscle damage:** to create muscle damage, there is a balance between volume and intensity of load. There needs to be enough volume at a high enough intensity to induce muscle damage and the subsequent adaptive responses to stimulate an increase in muscle mass.
3. **Metabolic stress:** the training stimulus must be able to place the musculature under metabolic stress, with metabolic stress being an accumulation of metabolites such as lactate and hydrogen ions. Increases in these metabolites suggest anaerobic lactic acid system stimulation is required (circa 60–120 seconds).

Knowing these three mechanisms provides the S&C coaches with explicit details of how best to stimulate the adaptive process for increases in muscle mass. This makes the process more deliberate and provides greater flexibility of the methods used to stimulate these three mechanisms. The full article is worth reading and can be downloaded for free from the publishers.

RELATIONSHIP TO ROWING PERFORMANCE

There are specific times when having an increased lean muscle mass can be advantageous for rowers. It is important to specifically identify how this may benefit rowing performance. Often the increase in the lean muscle mass will not lead directly to performance enhancement. It is what the increased lean muscle mass will allow the rower to do thereafter which will be performance enhancing. Indiscriminate increases in lean muscle mass can be detrimental to performance. Firstly, an increase in mass that does not functionally contribute to the rower's ability to increase boat speed is mass that the rower and crew must 'carry' while racing. This is dead weight requiring an increase in energy expenditure and force expression rather than contributing to the performance. Secondly, spending time on increasing unnecessary lean muscle mass is time not spent on developing other qualities necessary to contribute to performance. This may dampen the performance output, as these other important qualities may not have the necessary focus to fully contribute to the overall performance.

Typical examples of where an increase in lean muscle mass is required and hypertrophy training has been employed have been the reconditioning of rowers post-injury or those who would benefit from increased lean muscle mass to allow for an increased potential in force production (more lean muscle mass equates to greater density of muscle fibre: more muscle fibre has a greater potential to produce a larger force expression), when lightweight rowers transition into the openweight class or increase trunk musculature to support the spine from the forces it must manage. Increases in lean muscle mass may also be required post-enforced mobilization of a body segment leading to a gradual decrease of the lean muscle (atrophy) during the period of inactivity.

The identification of how an increase in lean muscle mass may positively impact performance requires collaboration between the rower, coaches and supporting staff. If the increase in mass is identified as an outcome, all parties must adequately allow for this adaptation to occur. Hypertrophy training cannot simply be added to the existing programme and must be carefully planned to ensure the outcome of increased lean muscle mass is achieved. Making significant changes in increased muscle mass can be extremely difficult, especially when there is a high degree of endurance-biased training being completed concurrently. This is why it simply cannot be added without something being taken away, which requires the coaches to understand the reasoning for completing this type of training, how long it will take and what modifications are required within the entire training process to allow hypertrophy training to be effectively prescribed and completed to attain the intended outcome.

Athlete Case Study

In the previous two chapters, the programmes shared are those of a rower, Chris Boddy. Having coached Chris for a number of years as a lightweight rower in the British Rowing programme, he made the decision to leave. He was struggling to maintain a body mass suitable for lightweight rowing (crew average weight of 70kg, with no single rower above 72.5kg). Chris is 188cm (approximately 6ft, 1in), which is tall for a lightweight making it hard to maintain a low body mass within the lightweight category. Chris made the decision to transition into the openweight category. As the name suggests, rowers can be any body mass to compete in this category. Chris left the programme and returned to club rowing with an aspiration to compete and win as an openweight in the prestigious Grand Challenge Cup at Henley Royal Regatta (HRR) a year later.

Table 8.1 highlights the changes Chris was required to achieve. To be competitive in the openweight category, male rowers should be able to complete a 2,000m rowing ergometer assessment in less than 6 minutes with the world record close to 5 minutes, 35 seconds. For Chris to get to the 6-minute mark, he would need to improve by almost 17 seconds. Chris's 2,000m personal best at the time was set as a lightweight weighing approximately 71–72kg. To get close to the 6-minute mark, Chris would need to significantly increase the volume of muscle mass, which could contribute force production during the task. Some basic calculations estimated Chris would need to increase lean body mass by approximately 12–13kg, with a total body mass of approximately 85kg. To ensure the increase in mass was functional (so would contribute to force production), an increase in countermovement jump mechanical peak power of approximately 1,500W would need to occur. A further marker of relative peak power to body mass was determined. This marker would assess the magnitude of mechanical peak power produced per kilo of body mass. An estimated increase of 5–6W.kg-1 would be required. Increases of absolute mechanical peak power without significant changes in relative mechanical peak power would suggest the increases in mass were not functionally contributing enough to performance.

Chris had a little over a year to prepare for the HRR. As previously discussed in Chapter 1 and throughout the book, a performance backwards approach is required with full alignment of the entire team supporting the rower. To make these changes would require signifi-

Table 8.1 Performance objectives to achieve 6-minute 2,000m ergometer performance

Performance Marker	Initial Assessment	Benchmark	Change Required
2000m Ergometer (M:S.MS)	06:16.9	06:00.0	00:16.9
Body Mass (kg)	73.0	85.0	12.0
CMJ Mechanical Absolute Peak Power (Watts)	5843	7343	1500
CMJ Mechanical Relative Peak Power (W.kg-1)	80.0	86.4	6.4

cant modifications to the training programme to allow Chris to optimally adapt. This would include the reduction of any aerobic endurance training; this would be required to be kept to a minimum. There would be a need to increase the number of hypertrophy-biased training sessions throughout the week. Without the coach understanding the demands of the intended outcome, it would be very challenging to reduce the aerobic training and increase hypertrophy training. It simply cannot be added to an already existing programme. There is not enough time in the week to complete it all; there would be an increase in workload and therefore stress on the rower and finally the adaptive response would be blunted, resulting in little to no adaptation, rendering the training completed worthless. Careful planning was needed to give Chris the opportunity to make significant changes early in the training programme as the management of total training could easily be done with little competition or heavy training camps. As the programme progressed, targeted periods were provided to make changes around the training plan. Providing insights of how training is progressing, and the inclusion of assessments provided all involved with updates on the development, with the next phases of training being modulated to meet both the needs of the rower and the demands of the event.

Table 8.2 highlights the actual changes made by the end of the programme. Chris managed to take over 15 seconds off the 2,000m ergometer performance. While this was not the 6-minute marker planned, it is still an incredible improvement. The body mass was 2.5kg over the expected target at 87.5kg. The changes in absolute and relative mechanical peak power were probably the most impressive. A 2,000W increase is the single largest change observed during this assessment of any athlete assessed. The relative mechanical peak power improvement was also significant. It was this marker which transitioned Chris's programme from a hypertrophy-biased programme to a heavy strength and explosive strength-training programme. After about 25 weeks, Chris's body mass was starting to stabilize at around 85–87kg. The absolute mechanical peak power had made significant changes with around 900W improvement. However, relative mechanical peak power dropped from 80W.kg-1 to 76.5W.kg-1. This observation suggested the increase in mass was not contributing to the performance outcome. The anthropometric measurements (see section 'Assess Change') showed the increase in mass was predominantly lean mass. The hypothesis was that the musculature had only really been subjected to hypertrophy training and would benefit from exposure to heavy strength and explosive strength training to increase the maximal force expression and rate of force development (RFD). Over the next 15–20 weeks, Chris was exposed to this type of training. The significant changes in absolute and relative mechanical peak power occurred from this point onwards with small changes in body mass resulting in the final assessment data in

Table 8.2 Performance objectives progression during training programme

Performance Marker	Initial Assessment	Final Assessment	Progression
2000m Ergometer (M:S.MS)	06:16.9	06:01.8	00:15.1
Body Mass (kg)	73.0	87.5	14.5
CMJ Mechanical Absolute Peak Power (Watts)	5843	7894	2051
CMJ Mechanical Relative Peak Power (W.kg-1)	80.0	90.2	10.2

Table 8.2. Chris did go on to win the Grand Challenge Cup at HRR. This is a testament to Chris's patience and perseverance to undertake such a transformation, which placed Chris in a position to perform competitively and win in the openweight category.

ASSESS CHANGE

There have been several occasions when speaking with S&C coaches, they have stated that the intended outcome of a training programme is increase in muscle mass. When asked what changes are expected and how those changes will be assessed, the replies suggest that the tracking of changes has not been carefully considered. This is probably one of the more challenging neuromuscular qualities to assess change as it requires specialized equipment and for some methods, specific training. However, if there is a deliberate attempt to increase muscle mass, how these changes will be assessed must be considered during the planning.

Anthropometrics

If increase in muscle mass is required, and with lack of any equipment, the simplest method is to weigh the rower. While this will only give you total body mass and cannot differentiate between changes in body tissues, it will provide a fundamental basis to work from. As described in Chapter 6, all assessments have a degree of variability, which this simple assessment is also susceptible to. Dehydration and sweat loss in cloth for example will bias the measurement. However, careful planning and organizing of assessments can mitigate these variables.

To gain greater insights into changes in muscle mass, having practitioners who are Level 1 accredited through the International Society for the Advancement of Kinanthropmetry (ISAK) will provide greater depth of understanding of where the changes in body mass have potentially occurred. Assessing skinfolds, which is a measure of body fat, and combining this with the girth of the body segment (combined lean muscle, fat and bone) can provide evidence of changes in both lean muscle and maintenance or reduction in body fat. While these are still crude measures of true change, they are a good proxy for body mass changes. As with weighing body mass, these methods are susceptible to the same variables, with the addition of user technique error. While these can be mitigated to some degree, when reporting this data back, it is worth always highlighting what factors are potentially affecting the data. Those looking to understand the training required for this method, please refer to the ISAK website (http://www.isakonline.com).

As discussed in Chapter 7, there is a trade-off between ease of use, cost and accuracy. While these methods have an initial outlay of costs and training, they are cheaper than alternative methods and give a degree of reliability. Measuring skinfolds and girths is time consuming if there is only one skilled practitioner to complete an entire squad. However, not all rowers may require regular monitoring. It is a fairly simple process to regularly provide for a small number of rowers if body mass changes need monitoring.

Alternative Methods

There are a number of other available methods that may be useful. However, some of these are more likely found in medical institutions and have significantly greater cost to them. The degree of accuracy is higher and may actually be easier and quicker to use. For example, Dual-energy X-ray absorptiometry (DEXA) has been shown to have a high degree of accuracy. The cost of a single use is circa £50–200 per session. For a squad of forty rowers, that makes it cost prohibitive, even on the lower side of the range. There are cheaper alternatives such as bio-impedance systems. This system passes low-frequency electrical currents through the body by gripping a handle and standing barefoot on a scale-like device. It measures the rate of electrical current knowing different body tissues (such as muscle and fat) conduct electrical currents at varying rates. While this technology has developed and become more accurate over the last fifteen years, there is a degree of inaccuracy similar to that discussed in the anthropometrics section; hydration and electrolyte status can alter the results.

As always there is a trade-off to have between cost, ease and accuracy. That said, all of these methods have a medium to high degree of reliability, so the ability to repeat the assessment within a rowing population will still provide useful insights to inform decision-making.

PROGRAMME GUIDELINES

Based on the mechanisms of increasing muscle through hypertrophy training outlined earlier, the following programmes are examples known to create the intended outcome. While the programmes may target one of the three mechanisms, as already established in Chapters 5 and 6, single adaptive processes cannot be targeted without other processes being stimulated. The programmes are biased towards a preferential adaptive response but recognize that many adaptive processes may be simultaneously stimulated. This is not a negative, as the intended outcome is still being met.

Mechanical Tension Biased

As discussed earlier, mechanical tension requires a high near maximal loading to stimulate a muscle mass increase adaptive response. Fig. 8.1 highlights a programme biased towards mechanical tension, using cluster sets. The rower will lift the first prescribed group of repetitions, rest for 10 seconds, lift the second group of prescribed repetitions and rest again for 10 seconds. Continue this process of lifting and recovering until all groups of repetitions are completed, with 2–3 minutes between each cluster set. The exercises selected have been chosen to provide a degree of safety. This type of training will result in rowers failing a set. It is safer with exercises where the rower is not likely to be trapped or injured if a failure occurs (for example, squatting and bench pressing would place rowers at high risk if a failure occurred). The load selected is around 80 per cent of the load a rower can lift for the

	Week 1		Week 2		Week 3		Week 4	
	Sets x Reps	% 1RM	Sets x Reps	% 1RM	Sets x Reps	% 1RM	Sets x Reps	% 1RM
Leg Press	6 x 10, 8, 5, 3	>87%	6 x 3, 5, 8, 10	>70%	6 x 5, 4, 3, 2, 1	>80%	6 x 1, 2, 3, 4, 5	>80%
Seated Row	6 x 10, 8, 5, 3	>70%	6 x 3, 5, 8, 10	>70%	6 x 5, 4, 3, 2, 1	>80%	6 x 1, 2, 3, 4, 5	>80%

Complete first group of repetitions, 10 seconds recovery, repeating this process until all groups of repetitions are completed within the set

Fig. 8.1 Mechanical tension-biased hypertrophy training programme.

MUSCLE AND TENDON MASS

	Week 1		Week 2		Week 3		Week 4	
	Sets x Reps	% 1RM	Sets x Reps	% 1RM	Sets x Reps	% 1RM	Sets x Reps	% 1RM
Leg Press	4 × 10	>75%	4 × 10	>75%	4 × 12	>70%	4 × 12	>70%
+ Single Leg Press*	4 × failure		4 × failure		4 × failure		4 × failure	
Trap Bar Deadlift	4 × 10	>75%	4 × 10	>75%	4 × 12	>70%	4 × 12	>70%
+ Leg Extension*	4 × failure		4 × failure		4 × failure		4 × failure	
Bench Press	4 × 10	>75%	4 × 10	>75%	4 × 12	>70%	4 × 12	>70%
+ Tricep Pull Down*	4 × failure		4 × failure		4 × failure		4 × failure	
Seated Row	4 × 10	>75%	4 × 10	>75%	4 × 12	>70%	4 × 12	>70%
+ Bicep Curl*	4 × failure		4 × failure		4 × failure		4 × failure	

*Exercises to be completed as a superset with the previous exercise

Fig. 8.2 Muscle damage-biased hypertrophy training programme.

large repetition group prescribed. For example, using week one leg press, if Chris could lift 400kg for 10 repetitions, a load of 320kg would be prescribed (80 per cent of 400kg).

Muscle Damage Biased

Muscle damage requires a balance between volume and intensity. The training programme Fig. 8.2 is biased towards muscle damage. The main exercise is completed, which is immediately followed by a superset to increase the local volume with a load at a high enough intensity. It is difficult to prescribe percentages of maximum repetition for this type of training. There is a degree of trial and error for the superset. The general rule of thumb is that the rower should only be able to lift between 12–18 repetitions to failure. If the rower is lifting less than 12 repetitions, lighten the load. If the rower is lifting greater than 18 repetitions, increase the load. This repetition window provides a load great enough and enough volume to create muscle damage. It may also contribute to the third mechanism of metabolic stress too. The rower will not rest between completing the exercise and its superset, but should take 2–3 minutes recovery between each set.

Metabolic Stress Biased

Metabolic stress refers to the accumulation of metabolites so anaerobic lactic acid system stimulation is required. This often occurs between circa 60–120 seconds with high intensity loading. Fig. 8.3 highlights the programming to best stimulate this adaptive response. Chris completed between 15–20 repetitions per set using a tempo of 202 to 303; 2–3 seconds on the initial lifting movement and 2–3 seconds returning the load to the start/finish position. For 15 repetitions, this would equate to 60–90 seconds of work. For 20 repetitions, this would equate to 80–120 seconds of work. The tempo is used for two reasons:

85

MUSCLE AND TENDON MASS

1. Increase the work accumulation within a set.
2. The tempo ensures the rower is using muscle contractions and not inertial movements to lift the prescribed loads, making sure the musculature has continual mechanical tension.

Between sets, rowers recover for 2–3 minutes.

To make significant increases in muscle mass, hypertrophy training should be completed 2–6 times a week. With a sport like rowing where there is a high degree of endurance-biased training and typically inexperienced lifters, the hypertrophy training stimulus needs to be quite high to make required changes. Experience has shown rowers are able to tolerate high volumes of training load. With the metabolic stress and muscle damage mechanisms, rowers may need to experience higher volume or manipulate recovery time to optimize the adaptive process, more so than other cohorts of athletes. Unlike heavy strength and explosive strength training, there is prescription of sets and repetitions and more bias around finding the method to optimize the stimulation of the adaptive mechanisms. Being too prescriptive may actually diminish the adaptive response. As highlighted with the case study above, significant changes can take anywhere from 5–30 weeks or even longer. Knowing how much change is required and how much time is available will help inform the decision-making process of what is achievable.

General Considerations

Concurrent training can be described as the simultaneous training of two divergent intended outcomes.[5] Rowers clearly need to have strong aerobic endurance capabilities to effectively perform.[6] It is equally important rowers have anaerobic neuromuscular capabilities.[7] These qualities are often trained within the same day or week. Training both these qualities simultaneously within this timeframe may result in confliction of adaptive responses. There is plenty of evidence to suggest endurance performance or adaptation is not negatively affected by the introduction of neuromuscular-biased training.[8] It can actually be endurance performance enhancing.[9,10] However, this may not be the case for neuromuscular performance and adaptation when aerobic endurance-biased training is introduced. Aerobic endurance training can blunt the neuromuscular adaptive responses, reducing the capability of the musculature to increase in size, exert maximal force and of RFD.[11] This is typically called the interference effect, where one adaptive process from a

	Week 1		Week 2		Week 3		Week 4	
	Sets x Reps	% 1RM	Sets x Reps	% 1RM	Sets x Reps	% 1RM	Sets x Reps	% 1RM
Deadlift	4 × 15	>70%	4 × 18	>67%	4 × 20	>60%	4 × 15	>70%
Leg Press	4 × 15	>70%	4 × 18	>67%	4 × 20	>60%	4 × 15	>70%
Bench Press	4 × 15	>70%	4 × 18	>67%	4 × 20	>60%	4 × 15	>70%
Seated Row	4 × 15	>70%	4 × 18	>67%	4 × 20	>60%	4 × 15	>70%

Fig. 8.3 Metabolic stress-biased hypertrophy training programme.

training stimulus interferes with another adaptive process from a concurrent training stimulus. In this case, it is neuromuscular adaptation and performance that is negatively impacted. This can render neuromuscular-biased training ineffective.

Organizing training becomes paramount with concurrent training. Rowers will often train 2–3 times a day and between 10–16 times a week, with the vast majority of training being aerobic endurance biased. The training plan is most often created by the chief coach so where neuromuscular-biased training is placed may already be pre-selected. That said, working from a performance backwards approach should provide a discussion with all the staff around the prioritization of training methods and planning against the intended outcome. With specific reference to increases in muscle mass, if hypertrophy training becomes a priority, changes to the entire training programme are required to provide optimal adaptation. The number of hypertrophy sessions may need to be as many as six a week with a significant reduction in total aerobic endurance training during this period. If this cannot be agreed, increase in muscle mass is not a priority and any attempt to do so will be futile. Only when there is prioritization will a programme adapt to meet this intended outcome.

Within a training day, when there is concurrent training, training should be spaced out to allow adequate recovery before completing the next training session. Experience has shown that neuromuscular adaptation and performance seems to be greatest when this is completed as either the first or last session of the day (assuming there are three sessions within a day). Having this session in the middle, sandwiched between aerobic endurance-biased sessions anecdotally seems to be the least effective planning. If neuromuscular training is completed in the last session, this will be the last adaptive response of the day and provides 14–16 hours between the next training stimulus. If it is the first session of the day, there has been the longest period of recovery from the last session of the day before, potentially meaning the rower is less fatigued when completing the session. Either way, equal success has been had with being the first or last session.

It is also worth making a small note on nutrition. The general rule with all training, but especially true with concurrent training is to:

1. **Refuel:** Ensure the rower consumes enough clean calories to replace the energy used within the training session. This will mean the rower does not start the next training session under-fuelled.
2. **Rehydrate:** Ensure the rower replaces lost fluids from training through water or electrolyte fluids, so that the hydration status does not creep into a dehydrated state for the next training session.
3. **Rebuild:** Ensure the rower consumes high-quality protein post-training sessions to optimize the adaptive process for both aerobic endurance and neuromuscular-biased training. This will avoid atrophy (loss of muscle mass), which occurs when there is not enough protein consumed. Low protein intake will also blunt adaptive responses so it is imperative that all rowers consume enough throughout the day.

It is beyond the scope of this chapter to provide detailed nutritional advice. However, Chapter 11 in *Training for the Complete Rower: A guide for improving your performance*[12] provides an excellent resource around nutrition for rowing.

CONCLUSION

Not every rower will require increases in muscle mass. However, for those who do, there are several considerations to make including how it will fit within the programme and whether all staff are aligned to the intended outcome. While increases in muscle mass may not have a direct impact on performance, it is what the increase in mass can provide that will support performance. The case study of Chris Boddy clearly demonstrated that simply increasing muscle mass did not automatically transfer into changes in performance. It was only when the newly created mass was given the opportunity to express its maximal force expression and RFD that it was able to start having significant contribution to performance. As with all the neuromuscular qualities within this book, it is important to identify the intended outcome and determine how long it will take along with the most effective methods to achieve this. If significant increases in muscle mass are required, give it time and space within the programme to happen and ensure the hypertrophy training is deliberate.

REFERENCES

1. De Pree, M. (2004). *Leadership is an Art*. New York, USA: Crown Publishing Group.
2. Bompa, T. O., & Buzzichelli, C. A. (2018). *Periodization: Theory and Methodology of Training*. Champaign, Illinois, USA: Human Kinetics.
3. *Ibid*.
4. Schoenfeld, B. J. (2010). The Mechanisms of Muscle Hypertrophy and their Application to Resistance Training. *Journal of Strength and Conditioning Research*. 24: 2,857–72.
5. Nader, G. A. (2006). Concurrent Strength and Endurance Training: From molecule to man. *Medicine and Science in Sport and Exercise*. 38, 1,965–70.
6. Secher, N. H. (1993). Physiological and Biomechanical Aspects of Rowing: Implications for training. *Sports Medicine*. 15, 24–42.
7. *Ibid*.
8. Nadar (2006).
9. *Ibid*.
10. Stone, M. H., Stone, M. E., Sands, W., Pierce, K. C., Newton, R. U., Haff, G. G., & Carlock, J. (2006). Maximum Strength and Strength Training – A relationship to endurance? *Strength and Conditioning Journal*. 28, 44–53.
11. Nadar (2006).
12. Thompson, P., & Wolf, A. (2015). *Training for the Complete Rower: A guide to improving your performance*. Wiltshire, UK: The Crowood Press.

9 | WORK CAPACITY

Nicole Chase

Without labour, nothing prospers

Sophocles[1]

DEFINING WORK CAPACITY

Within S&C coaching practice, there are numerous terms that appear to similarly describe 'work capacity', along with a vast array of definitions. The following terms could be mistaken to describe work capacity:

- tissue capacity
- tissue resilience
- muscle capacity
- muscle endurance
- local muscular endurance
- robustness
- tissue conditioning
- strength endurance.

It can therefore be difficult to align on terminology and a definition as an S&C cohort, when so much variation is present within the practice. This chapter will go through the underlying training adaptations that support rowing performance for the outcome of work capacity.

Work capacity will be defined as, 'the ability to produce or tolerate variable intensities and durations of work and contributes to the ability of an athlete to perform efficiently in a given sport'.[2] Therefore, work capacity is an outcome to support the training required to underpin the sport's performance outcome. Changes in work capacity will increase the ability of the muscular and energy systems to produce more work during repeated efforts, allowing the local musculature to tolerate or demonstrate resilience to a larger training volume of work, and support the performance of work closer to the intensity and duration required for sporting performance.

Work can be described as the ability to produce force over a given distance and is measured by force multiplied by distance in Newton-Metres (Nm).[3] A rower needs to complete a large amount of work to move a boat, which can be measured as force (the force exerted on the spoon of the oar through the handle) multiplied by distance (the distance the oar has travelled through the water) and is measured in Newtons per metre (Nm). The International System of Units (SI) describes work as the 'transfer of energy'[4], where energy is measured in Joules (J). Therefore, if the amount of work that can be produced is governed by the transfer of energy, then within the context of S&C, the transfer of energy can be influenced by volume (time/reps) and intensity (load on the bar). With these definitions in mind it is therefore important to note that the term 'work capacity' can be applied to anything from low-load, high-volume training, to high-load, low-volume training and covering everything in-between.

The production of work in the rowing stroke is underpinned by the rower's maximal force expression, which has been previously defined as 'the largest force the musculature can produce'.[5] An increase in a rower's maximal force, developed by maximal strength training, will improve their ability to apply force to the boat in the correct rowing technical postures. It is therefore the role of the S&C coach to develop the maximal force of the rower at the targeted muscular sites relative to the rowing stroke.

Impacting force characteristics can be local or global. An example of a 'local' force refers to a single joint, peripheral muscular structure such as the posterior hip. Creating a change in local force at the posterior hip would result in the musculature of the posterior hip increasing extension force at the hip, whereas an example of 'global' changes in force would refer to increases in a multi-joint movement such as a one-repetition maximum (RM) of the back squat. (Chapter 6 explored this in greater detail.)

Force-producing capabilities of a muscle have been linked to increasing work capacity capabilities. A correlation analysis between press-up and bench press, plus supine pull and bench pull in high-performance rowers showed a very strong relationship. This demonstrates that the athletes with the best work capacity capabilities are also the strongest. Work capacity is especially important in the musculature of the hip abductors, hip adductors, lower back and mid-back. These muscles should be targeted to manage the high-risk injury sites of the lower back, hip and rib cage, due to the kinetics and kinematics of the rowing stroke. Where kinetics are the forces that produce, change or stop the motion of the boat and body, and kinematics describe this motion.

RELATIONSHIP TO ROWING PERFORMANCE

The changes identified above are critical for rowing performance for two reasons. To manage the high-risk injury sites from the repeated loading of the tissues due to the demands of the sport, and to improve mechanical efficiency brought about by repeatedly being able to hit key technical positions. Both these outcomes require the rowers to have a high work capacity ability from the specific musculature involved, for the duration of the 2,000m race.

When considering the demands of a rowing stroke and race, as discussed in recent chapters, it is important to reference that the rower's ability to not only produce large local forces but also repeatedly use a high percentage of this is an important physical characteristic for rowing performance. Although increases in force can be brought about through strength training, it is the combination of the increased ability to produce maximal force with the ability to repeatedly produce sub-maximal force that leads to improved rowing performance. It is also pertinent to ensure that training interventions are targeted towards the muscle groups most related to rowing performance, not only for minimizing the risk of injury due to repeated stress of these muscles but also for enhancing rowing performance. As described in previous chapters, the legs produce the most power per stroke in rowing (46.4 per cent), followed by the trunk, then the arms and shoulders.

As previously discussed, work capacity can be applied to anything from low-load, high-volume training, to high-load, low-volume training and covering everything in-between. However, the human body's energy system requirements to produce these repeated

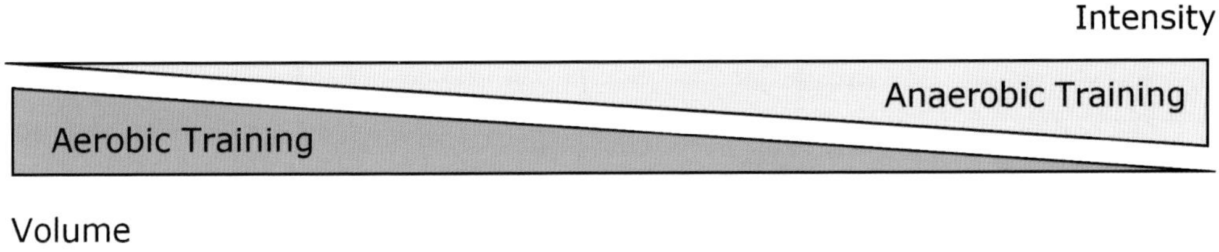

WORK CAPACITY

Intensity

Aerobic Training — Anaerobic Training

Volume

Fig. 9.1 Relationship between volume and intensity.

actions at high-load versus low-load conditions are very different with energy production coming from short anaerobic energy production vs long aerobic energy production respectively. Within the S&C context, work capacity is most commonly trained within the high-volume, low-load prescription but it could be of equal value to train within the high-load, low-volume context. However, by increasing an individual's maximal capability, the demands of the sport become relatively less intense.

The variables of volume and intensity have an impact on the body's energy systems from short anaerobic energy production (alactic < 6 seconds) to longer-lasting aerobic energy production (> 60 seconds). In an applied setting it is therefore useful to think of a work capacity training intervention and its associated training adaptations along the volume and intensity continuum (Fig. 9.1).

For a change in work capacity to have taken place, a suitable training window needs to have been completed with the appropriate volume, intensity and frequency. If you re-test too soon then you may not have accumulated enough training load to create a true change in work capacity. If the training prescription is correct, then a change in work capacity can be seen within 4–6 weeks. When this data is taken, however, relies on an understanding of not only the S&C programme but also the bigger picture rowing programme.

Due to the demands of rowing and the need to manage specific tissues that are exposed to repeated loading, the low-load, high-volume prescription is most commonly used to develop work capacity in a rower. The primary objective of this training is to increase general or specific physical capacity to allow for repeated loading in the weight room and the boat. Specifically, muscle protein synthesis (MPS) has been shown to be elevated post-low-load, high-volume resistance training, creating local adaptation to muscle with low biological cost.[6] Rehearsal of movement patterning can also be achieved, chronic local adaptation to the muscle and tendon[7], increases in metabolic function, defined as the processes needed to maintain a living organism, and strength endurance.

High-volume, low-load work capacity training can be used to help manage a high-risk injury site such as the rib cage, which can often be subject to rib stress injury, defined as 'the development of pain due to bone oedema caused by overload along the rib shaft'.[8] An exercise such as the plate pullover (Figs 9.2 and 9.3) can be used to target the serratus anterior to increase MPS, movement patterning and metabolic function in these local muscle tissues.

Increases in work capacity in the high-load, low-volume programme could be seen by completing more work in a given period, also referred to as increasing training density or by performing the same amount of work for longer, as in the example of a 2,000m rowing race. In the strength density example, the high-intensity stimulus will cause secondary adaptations in the following; increases in neurological factors such as motor unit recruitment, firing frequency, motor unit synchronization and intermuscular coordination.[9]

WORK CAPACITY

Fig. 9.2 Pullover start/finish position.

Fig. 9.3 Pullover bottom of descent position.

An example of such work capacity training would be 4–6 sets of back squats, completing 4–8 repetitions every minute on the minute. This type of protocol will be discussed further in the programming guidelines section of this chapter.

The third format of work capacity is moderate volume and moderate intensity training, where these variables of volume and intensity will cause secondary adaptations in morphological factors such as the following: cross-sectional area, muscle pennation angle, fascicle length and fibre type.[10] This is because the protocol of moderate volume and moderate intensity creates similar tissue stress to a bodybuilding programme that is targeting increases in hypertrophy. Chapter 8 provides more detail around hypertrophy mechanisms. This type of work capacity training in the rowing population has been seen to develop a good strength endurance base within the winter season, with secondary changes in arm girth using exercises such as the barbell bench pull.

ASSESSING CHANGE

It is very important for an S&C coach to understand the effectiveness of their S&C programmes and the subsequent changes that have been made on the athlete's work capacity. It is therefore imperative that pre- and post-testing is completed to ascertain the change in work capacity and whether this met what was required for the athlete. To truly understand whether the change in work capacity has been meaningful, the reliability of the testing needs to first be understood. This can be done by working out the test error and therefore what a meaningful change is above that. This is important because if the test error is three repetitions, then the athlete must have moved on by at least four repetitions for the change to be meaningful.

When selecting a re-testing window, it is important to ascertain the amount of rowing loading that is being completed at the same time and whether the athletes are building towards a performance piece. The changes in training from the main rowing programme can influence the results of your testing, especially if the athletes are in a heavy rowing training block where a large amount of fatigue will be present. The above should be taken into consideration not only when you're planning your re-testing window but also with how you interpret the results. Due to the hours of training required to create a change in aerobic capacity, it is unlikely that there will be windows to re-test for work capacity changes when the rowing demand is low. This means that the athletes will nearly always be under

WORK CAPACITY

Trunk Capacity (Seconds)

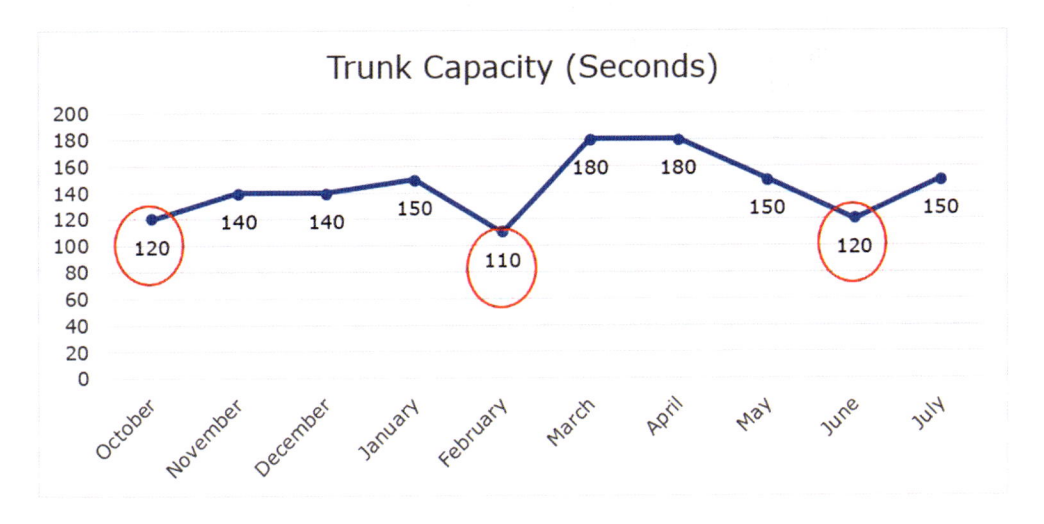

[Chart showing monthly values: October 120, November 140, December 140, January 150, February 110, March 180, April 180, May 150, June 120, July 150. October, February and June values are circled.]

Testing – If data for the above variable was only taken in Oct, Feb and June then a S&C practitioner may conclude that the athlete's work capacity in this test hadn't improved, as this is the information presented from the data.

Monitoring – By tracking the peaks and troughs of a training variable such as work capacity, the S&C practitioner can ascertain the improvements in the athlete's trunk capacity over the course of a season. This is because a monitoring approach considers the neuromuscular fatigue that may be present in the athlete's sytem, and hence influencing the above testing interpretation of the data.

Fig. 9.4 In-season changes in trunk capacity scores (Assessment versus Monitoring).

some form of fatigue or neuromuscular suppression, which will impact the results. The limited windows to accurately track change in physical markers lead the S&C coach to a monitoring rather than testing approach to assess changes in physical markers. Fig. 9.4 illustrates the differences between perceived changes in testing versus monitoring.

As can be seen from Fig. 9.4 there is a general increasing trend in the variable measured. However, if you only interpreted the data from October, January and March then you would think that the athlete would have either only maintained or in fact decreased their physicality in body weight pressing capacity. Even though there is a clear upward trend in the data, this is because there are periods when the athlete is fatigued, which will impact their work capacity. This information means the S&C coach should ensure there is a balance between regular monitoring of important work capacity variables versus only three time points per year where these variables are tested. How the monitoring is carried out will depend on the integration of the S&C coach and programme, with the rowing coach and main rowing programme. It is important that these programmes are mapped out together to ensure the monitoring windows are appropriate and aligned to the wider rowing programme objectives.

The in-training monitoring approach is also useful for tracking symmetry, which is important to measure in relation to managing high-risk injury sites. Symmetry can be tracked in several ways; left to right, anterior to posterior or lateral to medial and is specific to the athlete and their compensation patterns. Good symmetry in all planes of motion would fall into the ratio of 0.9–1.1, where a value outside of this range would be considered for a programming intervention. Athlete asymmetries in high performance rowers have been seen to increase during periods of high training volume where fatigue is high. It is important to 'catch these asymmetries' early, so that an intervention can be put into place if required to maintain the athlete at, or close to, their baseline. This is a discussion that should be had between the coach, physio and S&C coach to ascertain what path to take for the specified athlete.

PROGRAMMING GUIDELINES

High Volume, Low Intensity

When writing S&C programmes to change work capacity, some general variables need to be taken into consideration. In the example of high-volume, low-intensity work capacity training where the objective is to manage high-risk injury sites, such as the rib cage in rowing, then the following applies. The intensity should be low at around 30 per cent 1RM, with volume high at 4–6 sets of 15–20 repetitions or 6–10 minutes of 60 seconds. The weekly frequency should be high at around 4–6 times per week, to ensure a consistent stimulus and time-course for MPS. The use of tempo in high–volume, low–load training is also an excellent method to increase muscle tension, increasing MPS. Table 9.1 provides training prescription guidelines for high–volume, low–intensity programming.

This type of training requires little or no recovery, as the biological cost is very low. Therefore, a circuit of exercises could be run with 30–60 seconds recovery at the end of the circuit. Exercises should always be through full range and under control. Table 9.2 provides an example circuit focused on high-volume, low-load work capacity training.

Moderate Volume, Moderate Intensity

At the point where both volume and intensity are moderate, more recovery is needed,

Table 9.1 An example of high-volume, low-intensity training prescription

Outcome	Loading	Volume	Intensity	Frequency	Tempo
Tissue tolerance*	Work capacity	High	Low	High	Yes

*Where tissue tolerance is described as the ability to produce or tolerate increased intensities and durations of work.

Table 9.2 An example of a high-volume, low-intensity work capacity circuit

Exercise	Time	Load at 202 Tempo
Hip Bridge	60s	20kg
Pullovers	60s	10kg
Sumo Squat	60s	15kg
Bent Over Row	60s	15kg
Rest x 60 seconds	Repeat above	

Table 9.3 An example of moderate volume, moderate intensity training prescription

Outcome	Loading	Volume	Intensity	Frequency	Tempo
Metabolite accumulation	Work capacity	Moderate	Moderate	Moderate	Possible

as the biological cost of the prescription is much higher. Here the intensity will be around 40–60 per cent 1RM and volume between 10–20 repetitions with a work to rest ratio of around 1:1. This work to rest ratio creates incomplete recovery and therefore greater metabolic stress, which results in the subsequent build-up of metabolites.[11] Due to the increased biological cost, this type of work capacity training would only be required 3–4 times a week, as opposed to the 4–6 times in the low-load, high-volume prescription. Table 9.3 provides an example session focusing on moderate volume and intensity work capacity training.

An example of moderate volume and intensity training in this work capacity zone for bench pull:

- 6 sets of 15 repetitions
- 45 seconds recovery
- 60 per cent of 1 Repetition Maximum (1RM).

This type of work capacity training is especially useful for endurance athletes such as rowers, as their base levels of aerobic capacity mean as a population of athletes they can produce, tolerate and sustain high volumes of submaximal workloads, which is specific to the demands of their event. The specific adaptations of this type of training do however reduce during the periods where work capacity training in this zone isn't present. Therefore, this type of work capacity training is most useful closer to racing, unless the secondary outcome of hypertrophy is required during an earlier stage of the season.

Low Volume, High Intensity

The final zone to discuss is where volume is low, but intensity is high. During these demands the biological cost is very high and so recovery should reflect these needs, with a work to rest ratio closer to 1:2 or 1:3. The frequency should be 2–3 times a week to reflect the biological cost on the system. See Table 9.4 for the low volume, high intensity training prescription.

An example of this type of work capacity training for the back squat:

- 4–6 sets of 4–8 repetitions every minute
- remainder of minute as recovery
- 70–80 per cent of 1 Repetition Maximum (1RM).

The low-volume, high-intensity approach to developing work capacity can be used to complete more work in a given period, also referred to as an increased training density, or by performing the same amount of work for longer, as in the example of a 2,000m rowing race.

Table 9.4 Low-volume, high-intensity training prescription

Outcome	Loading	Volume	Intensity	Frequency	Tempo
Metabolite accumulation	Work capacity	Low	High	Low	No

Programming Considerations

It is important to note the three different types of protocol for the same training outcome of work capacity. Understanding the adaptations you are trying to change directs the prescription and ultimately the success of the S&C programme. Therefore, it is important to understand the specifics of work capacity under the above conditions for the greatest programme effect.

In a similar way to assessing change, it is important that the S&C programme maps to the rowing programme to ensure the greatest chance of adaptation. A high-performance rower can complete up to three sessions a day, so it is imperative that they rest and refuel between each session to get the most out of the next session. Periods of high volume or intensity in the weight room and the rowing programme at the same time should be kept to a minimum to reduce the incidence of competing adaptations and the risk of overtraining. The role of planning the programme with the rowing coach is of the utmost importance to ensure the S&C and rowing programmes are aligned in their objectives and given the greatest chance to obtain the specified adaptations.

In the low-intensity, high-volume work capacity prescription the frequency should be high, which is often difficult to achieve in a high-performance rowing programme, when aerobic training demands are also very high. This dose of work capacity training does not always need to be completed within the weight room sessions and could be completed at a separate or additional point within the day. For example, the scenario of a 'top-up' dose of trunk capacity after the first session of the day could be introduced 3–5 times a week to maximize the chance of tissue tolerance adaptations. These 8–10 minute 'top-up' doses, combined with the doses of the same stimulus within the S&C programme, will create the best opportunity for adaptation in this area.

PRINCIPLES

Better Conditioned Athletes have Greater Force Characteristics

This may sound like an obvious statement, but observations are that athletes that are not well conditioned struggle to withstand the demands of training loads required to significantly change force characteristics. Evidence of this has been demonstrated numerous times with different athlete populations. For example, there is a strong relationship between the maximum bench press load and number of press-ups to failure. Again, it may seem obvious that if an athlete has a higher maximum bench press load, a single press-up will be a lower percentage of maximum bench press load. Therefore, this athlete should be able to complete more press-up repetitions than those who have a lower maximum bench press load where a single press-up is at a higher percentage of maximum bench press load.

However, what if this was observed in reverse? The ability of an athlete to lift larger loads is because the athlete can not only complete more repetitions but also withstand higher training loads, which provide the opportunity to develop force characteristics. The relationship is an important one to consider. How often are athletes observed struggling to complete and tolerate higher intensity loading? These athletes tend to have lower than average loads when compared to the squad average load. When comparing these athletes to athletes with above average loads, these athletes can complete and tolerate higher-intensity-based loading. This is observational and not necessarily evidenced.

However, statistical analysis completed on several squads demonstrated that if an athlete demonstrated a poor work capacity assessment based on maximum time or repetition tasks, that athlete would have poor work capacity across all assessed areas. An athlete that demonstrated a high degree of work capacity from an assessment would have high work capacity across all assessed areas. This suggests that athletes tend to fall into either high work capacity, average work capacity or poor work capacity. While no analysis was completed to determine if weight room performances were also associated with work capacity, observationally, it would seem that athletes would fall into the respective groups (higher work capacity and higher maximal loading, average work capacity and average maximal loading and poor work capacity and poor maximal loading). Based on this, the development of work capacity is an important consideration in the development of force characteristics. While work capacity may not have a direct link to performance, it is a supplementary to characteristics that are directly linked to performance.

REFERENCES

1. Kirov, B. (2016). *Sophocles: Quotes and Facts*. California, USA: CreateSpace Independent Publishing Platform Location.
2. Spencer, S., Wolf, A., & Rushton, A. (2016). Spinal-Exercise Prescription in Sport: Classifying Physical Training and Rehabilitation by Intention and Outcome. *Journal of Athletic Training*. 51, 613–28.
3. Hamill, J. A. (2015). Biomechanical Basis of Human Movement. In K. A. Knutzen & T. R. A. Derrick (Eds.), *Human Movement* (Fourth ed.): Philadelphia, PA: Lippincott Williams & Wilkins.
4. *Ibid.*
5. Spencer *et al.* (2016).
6. Burd, N. A., West, D. W. D., Staples, A. W., Atherton, P. J., Baker, J. M., Moore, D. R., Holwerda, A. M., Parise, G., Rennie, M. J., Baker, S. K., & Phillips S. M. (2010). Low-Load High Volume Resistance Exercise Stimulates Muscle Protein Synthesis More Than High-Load Low Volume Resistance Exercise in Young Men (Exercise and Protein Synthesis). PLOS ONE. 5, e12033.
7. Spencer *et al.* (2016).
8. Evans, G., & Redgrave, A. (2016). Great Britain Rowing Team Guideline for Diagnosis and Management of Rib Stress Injury: Part 1. *British Journal of Sports Medicine*. 50, 266.
9. Cormie, M. P., McBride, O. J., & McCaulley, O. G. (2009). Power-Time, Force-Time, and Velocity-Time Curve Analysis of the Countermovement Jump: Impact of Training. *Journal of Strength and Conditioning Research*. 23, 177–86.
10. Cormie, P., McGuigan, M., & Newton, R. (2011). Developing Maximal Neuromuscular Power. *Sports Medicine*. 41, 17–38.
11. Schoenfeld, J. B. (2010). The Mechanisms of Muscle Hypertrophy and Their Application to Resistance Training. *Journal of Strength and Conditioning Research*. 24, 2,857–72.

10 STRENGTH AND CONDITIONING FOR PARALYMPIC ROWING

Tom Rusga

It's not disabilities, it's our abilities that count
Chris Burke[1]

INTRODUCTION

Para-rowing is rowing or sculling open to both male and female rowers with a disability who meet the criteria set out in the para-rowing classification regulations. Para-rowing was formerly called adaptive rowing and was first raced at the 2002 World Rowing Championships in Seville. It was introduced to the Beijing 2008 Paralympic Games for the first time and subsequently interest and participation has continued to grow. The Rio 2016 Paralympic Games had twenty-six countries competing in four boat classes with a total of forty-eight boats and ninety-six rowers.

In 2017, the race distance changed from 1,000m to 2,000m for all events. This is a considerable change in the demands of the event and has a greater relative influence on certain boat classes. For example, at the time of writing, the world's best in the PR1Wx is 10:13:630 whilst the world's best in the PR34+ is 06:55:700. Whilst this is important to acknowledge, all 2km rowing events maintain similar energetic demands despite the differences in event time. Therefore, for the purposes of this chapter the physiological and energetic demands of the sport will not be treated any differently to able-bodied rowing.

CLASSIFICATION

The International Rowing Federation (FISA) system of classification places rowers into classes according to the nature and extent to which their impairment impacts rowing and various boat classes are available for each classification (Table 10.1).

General Approach

Key principles in the early chapters of this book have shaped a philosophical approach to S&C as a performance support service. Specifically, that S&C is not the event itself and that a problem-solving approach that is rower-centred and works backwards from performance is necessary. The nature of some impairments may mean that certain physical constraints are less modifiable than would otherwise be encountered. However, the adherence to these key principles is no less important in a Paralympic setting. Therefore,

Table 10.1 FISA classification and available boat classes[2]

Classification	Description	Boat Classes	
PR3-PD	Rowers with a verifiable and permanent disability who have functional use of their legs, trunk and arms for rowing, and who can utilize the sliding seat to propel the boat.	PR3Mix2x PR3 M2- PR3 W2- **PR3Mix4+**	Mixed double scull Men's pair Women's pair **Mixed coxed four**
PR3-VI	Rower with 10% of vision in best eye with best correction and who have functional use of their legs, trunk and arms for rowing, and who can utilize the sliding seat to propel the boat.		
PR2	Rowers who have functional use of the trunk movement and who are unable to use the sliding seat to propel the boat because of significantly weakened function or mobility of the lower limbs.	PR2M1x PR2W1x **PR2Mix2x**	Men's single scull Women's single scull **Mixed double scull**
PR1	Rowers who have no or minimal trunk function. A PR1 class rower is able to apply force predominantly using the arms and/or shoulders. These rowers will also likely have decreased sitting balance.	**PR1M1x PR1W1x**	**Men's single scull Women's single scull**

Boat classes in normal text denote world championship events and those in bold denote world championship and Paralympic events.

understanding the impairment, as well as all other physical characteristics of the rower and how these relate to the mechanical demands of each boat class, is critical.

Understanding the Impairment

An exhaustive list of impairments is beyond the scope of this chapter and probably not practicable anyway. However, there are some common groups of impairments that are likely to be encountered by an S&C coach working with Paralympic rowers. By categorizing, the information herein is simplified and more comprehensible, but this belies the idiosyncratic and nuanced pathophysiology of each individual's impairment and its influence on their function. Two rowers with the same disability are unlikely to have the same severity of impairment, and the influence of the impairment is likely to manifest in a unique and individual manner. Therefore, it is imperative that the practitioner truly understands the individual as well as their disability and subsequent needs to provide more effective individual support.

Spinal Cord Injury (SCI)
Impairment of the spinal cord can occur due to traumatic injury, congenital disorder or specific illness/infection. Two critical factors that influence function following SCI are the lesion

level and completeness of the injury. The level of the lesion relates to where in the spinal cord the injury has occurred, this level will likely affect the corresponding nerve roots and all nerve roots distal to the injury. An incomplete lesion may allow some function of the neuromuscular system below the lesion, but this function is likely to be very specific to the individual. Conversely a complete lesion will often leave the individual with no voluntary contractions at the muscles innervated by the nerve roots below the lesion.

Limb Deficiency

Limb deficiency is an impairment group constituting rowers with an absence of bones or joints resulting from congenital limb deficiency or amputation following traumatic injury or vascular or bone pathologies.[3] These rowers are likely to use some sort of prosthesis or other assistive implement in either everyday life or during their training. Considering how this affects their movement and the subsequent loading their joints experience is important. For example, a unilateral below-knee amputee who uses a prosthetic leg is likely to have an altered gait which affects the habitual loading around all other joints. This may lead to increased capability through habitual loading in some vectors around certain joints and decreased ability in others.

Neurological Disorders

Neurological disorders can occur at any level (centrally or peripherally) or affect the entire nervous system (neurodegenerative disorders). The impairment can affect one limb (monoplegia), the lower limbs more than the upper body (diplegia), one side more than the other (hemiplegia) or all limbs (quadriplegia). In addition, the impairment can present in many ways including increased muscle tension (hypertonia), lack of coordinated contractions (ataxia) and/or abnormal involuntary contractions (athetosis).[4]

Exploring the detail of the disorder is critical and will help guide the S&C programme. For example, cerebral palsy (CP) is caused by abnormal development or injury to the parts of the brain that control movement. Therefore, whilst the dysfunction may manifest itself at the muscular level, it is driven by a physical/structural impairment at the level of the brain. The motor neurons are receiving an abnormal signal from the nervous system and the magnitude, rate and timing of contraction is impaired. Here, finding ways to overload the affected muscles, given that the voluntary contraction is impaired, may lead to further adaptation.

Visual Impairment

Rowers with a visual impairment can be either severely sight impaired (blind) or sight impaired (partially sighted). Whilst this could be combined with another impairment, that may not necessarily be the case and it will be discussed as a stand-alone impairment here. Typically, rowers with a visual impairment can be assessed and programmed for as an able-bodied rower would be. However, there are specific areas from a coaching perspective that should be considered and are discussed later in the chapter.

MECHANICAL DEMANDS

To move a boat quickly there are consistent mechanical demands that must be satisfied within the rower-boat-water system. A consistent principle across all classes is ensuring that the boat set-up and coached technique provide optimal leverage based on the level and nature of function of the rower/crew. Ensuring there is optimal mechanical advantage is essential to maximize force application. However, when examining just the rower within this system, due to the constraints of impairment and classification, the way in which the mechanical demands of rowing can be satisfied varies greatly between classes. Therefore,

STRENGTH AND CONDITIONING FOR PARALYMPIC ROWING

Fig. 10.1 PR1 rowing: thorax, shoulders and arms driven.

the demands between classes should be considered as different, independent tasks, rather than truncated versions of a full rowing stroke.

PR1 Mechanical Demands

PR1 rowers have no, or minimal, trunk function and are supported by a fixed leg position and strap around the abdomen. This means that the stroke is largely driven by the thorax, shoulders and arms (Fig. 10.1).

At the catch, PR1 rowers will demonstrate a considerable forward lean of the trunk. This is limited by abdominal strapping and subsequently, much of the forward lean comes from thoracic flexion. Following the catch, in order to accelerate the boat, a global trunk extension occurs. Again, due to the regulations around strapping, much of this extension occurs at the thoracic region. Following the onset of rapid trunk extension there is a coordinated 'pull' at the arms. This primarily involves shoulder extension and abduction, scapular retraction and depression as well as elbow flexion. Following this drive phase, the rower must decelerate and reaccelerate their body forward during the back turn before recycling during the recovery phase into the next stroke.

It is also noteworthy that due to the decreased stroke length, PR1 rowers typically train and perform at a marginally higher stroke rate than the other classifications and able-bodied rowers.

PR2 Mechanical Demands

PR2 rowers have functional use of the trunk but are unable to use the sliding seat due to significantly weakened function or mobility of the lower limbs. The rowers are supported by a fixed leg position but are free to move across the hip and trunk. This means that the stroke is largely driven by the hips and lumbar spine with additional work from the thorax, shoulders and arms (Fig. 10.2).

At the catch, PR2 rowers will demonstrate a considerable forward lean of the trunk. This comes primarily as a product of hip flexion but will likely also be associated with some global spinal flexion. Following the catch, in order to accelerate the boat, hip and trunk extension occur. The hip extension is likely to be driven by the hamstrings and posterior hip musculature whilst the extensors of the lumbar spine also create an extension torque. In addition, some PR2 rowers can press at the foot plate, so knee extension may also contribute to the net force generated. Following this rapid extension, the same coordinate 'pull' occurs

STRENGTH AND CONDITIONING FOR PARALYMPIC ROWING

Fig. 10.2 PR2 rowing: hips, lumbar spine, thorax, shoulders and arms driven.

as in the PR1 classification. The back turn and recovery phase are then typified by a traditional 'rockover' action before performing the next stroke.

It is also noteworthy that due to the decreased stroke length, PR2 rowers typically train and perform at a marginally higher stroke rate than PR3 and able-bodied rowers.

PR3 Mechanical Demands

PR3 rowers have functional use of their legs, trunk and arms for rowing, and can utilize the sliding seat to propel the boat. This means that, impairment aside, the rowing stroke is the same as for able-bodied rowers. Therefore, the mechanical demands will not be expounded upon further in this chapter.

UNDERSTANDING AND DECREASING RISK OF INJURY

Injury risk can be understood as a balance of a rower's capability to deal with the demands of a given task. Capability should be considered as a dynamic resource, and it's clear that the demands of a task can fluctuate and vary. A key step in understanding and subsequently decreasing injury risk is in accurately identifying the demands of a task and developing the specific physical capabilities to tolerate these demands.

PR1 Injury Risk

With the stroke being primarily driven by the thorax, shoulders and arms, the likely profile for injury risk for PR1 rowers is considerably different to the other Paralympic categories and able-bodied rowing.

Firstly, PR1s can be susceptible to chest wall injuries as a product of their strapping. Typically, this problem sits outside of the S&C coach's remit. However, strapping is not the only contributor to chest wall injuries and when it is, ensuring the rower has the appropriate trunk extension capabilities not to 'fall' into the strap too much and subsequently create excessive compression is important. In addition to this, ensuring that the rest of the upper body can generate enough force without the need for excessive movement of the ribs is essential.

Furthermore, due to the demands around the shoulder girdle, there is likely to be an increased risk of injury at this site and the neck.

PR1 rowers often demonstrate a noticeable forward head posture, anterior and superior positioning of the humeral head relative to the glenoid fossa and scapular elevation and protraction during the catch in order to increase stroke length. Generating force from this position is likely to be particularly taxing on the supporting contractile and non-contractile tissues and these structures should be prepared appropriately. The principles discussed in the preceding chapters (Chapters 6–9) can be applied to these structures to ensure they are adequately prepared.

As more force needs to be generated by the elbow flexors (biceps) in this category, the elbow may also be a site for concern. Particularly as although during the catch it may be desirable for the elbows to be in full extension whilst the force is generated, some rowers perform this position with a small amount of elbow flexion which has clear implications for the elbow flexor group such as biceps strains and elbow-related tendon and ligament injuries. Here, an appropriate magnitude and balance of elbow flexor and extensor force production is desirable.

Finally, due to the increased amount of pulling through the arms, forearm compartment syndrome is a common injury in this cohort. Ensuring other muscles are well enough developed to perform the required work and developing an adequate level of grip strength may mitigate against this.

PR2 Injury Risk

Rowers in this category perform the stroke with a largely hip and lumbar spine-driven action with additional work from the thorax, shoulders and arms.

Generating large hip and lumbar extension torques from a flexed hip and trunk position in order to accelerate the boat provides the primary biomechanical risk factor. Subsequently, developing the hip musculature as well as the contractile and non-contractile tissue that interacts with the lumbar spine is vital. Here, the nature of the impairments that rowers have that commonly compete in this category (SCI, limb deficiency and neurologic disorder) can provide an initial challenge in loading the hips and spine. For example, for a rower in this category with SCI, depending on the level and completeness of the injury, traditional strength-training exercises that load these tissues may not be appropriate. In this case, maintaining clarity about the physical capabilities required to mitigate against injury risk and flexibility in their solutions to creating adaptation in line with this is essential.

As with the PR1 category, chest wall, shoulder, neck, elbow and forearm injuries can occur, although seemingly with a smaller incidence, and should still be considered.

PR3 Injury Risk

Again, impairment aside, the biomechanical demands of PR3 rowing are the same as in able-bodied rowing. Here, as with all Paralympic rowers, the unique influence of the rower's impairment on function is the key component in understanding individual injury risk. For example, a rower with a single side lower-limb deficiency, such as a below-knee amputee, is unlikely to apply force at the foot plate symmetrically. They may also have an asymmetric general flexion range of movement on the affected side, which will have a significant impact on their ability to compress into the front turn. Subsequently, the forces occurring around the pelvis and spine are likely to be asymmetric and may increase the likelihood of pathology in this region.

DEVELOPING PHYSICAL CHARACTERISTICS TO IMPROVE PERFORMANCE

The mechanical demands of each category were described earlier in this chapter. Maximizing the magnitude of force that a rower can produce at a rate that is relevant for the stroke rate through these key positions and phases is key to impacting boat speed. Here, the principles discussed in Chapter 6 around developing maximal force expression can be used in conjunction with a clear understanding of the mechanical demands of each boat class to inform appropriate assessment protocols, as well as exercise selection and loading parameters when programming for adaptation.

When considering performance impact, a second consideration is ensuring that the force that is produced is applied in the most efficient manner through effective technique. This will ensure that as much force as possible that is generated is directed towards accelerating the boat and will decrease the relative energy demand. The relationship between changes in physical characteristics and changes in technique is beyond the scope of this chapter but should be based on a clear understanding of the coach's ambitions, biomechanics of rowing and motor control and skill development theories.

COACHING PARALYMPIC ROWERS

Coaching Paralympic rowers provides a unique challenge to the S&C coach. Clearly, the nature of these challenges is specific to the rowing group and in a para-rowing setting the coach may be working with rowers from all classifications within one session. In this case, due consideration to the organization and structure of the session is essential. This allows coaching to be distributed purposefully and ensures rowers get the most from the session.

Some rowers are likely to have limited mobility, meaning that coaching is quite 'hands on' in aiding transfer to and from equipment. It's worth acknowledging that this can create a certain sense of apprehension for coaches who have never worked with Paralympic rowers. Here, common sense should prevail in allowing the rower to guide the coach on the best approach and what assistance is and isn't required. Furthermore, some rowers may require the provision of greater stability (such as holding or strapping legs on the bench pull) to perform certain exercises effectively. Here, the coach must be sensitive to the rower's comfort, and again, following the rower's guidance is often the best approach.

Understandably, transferring onto and away from certain equipment can take time and considering this within session design is important. For example, a superset between the glute-ham raise and bench pull may require much of the coach's time and attention in facilitating the flow of the session with one rower, rather than adding value through effective coaching to all rowers. Considering all these factors during the planning process will allow a much smoother session flow where the coach can impart the appropriate technical delivery and motivational climate.

An often overlooked but noteworthy consideration is programming for and coaching visually-impaired rowers. Tackling this will be dependent on the extent and nature of the visual impairment but may require a considerably modified programme template, and/or the use of transcript-audio technology. One of the easiest solutions is for the rowers to have the programme on a tablet or phone in order to zoom in where necessary. Regardless, this experience will require a coach to communicate verbally with greater clarity and precision. Furthermore, when coaching, ensuring the removal of obstacles and creating an appropriate training space is imperative.

In summary, three things stand out in delivering effective coaching that is specific to Paralympic rowers. First, taking extra consideration of the logistical demands of the session and how this can be structured to afford the most effective coaching to be delivered is critical. Secondly, using common sense, demonstrating sensitivity and allowing the rowers to guide the coach are often the quickest ways to overcome practical challenges. Finally, where possible, maintaining a lower than normal rower to coach ratio is beneficial and helps maintain coaching quality.

CONCLUSION

In conclusion, whilst there are some areas that are specific to working with Paralympic rowers, such as understanding the impairment, the mechanical demands of each boat class and what that means for reducing injury risk and developing performance, the principles of effective coaching and S&C support remain. Firstly, that S&C is not the event itself and that a problem-solving approach that works backwards from performance and understands constraints is necessary. Finally, but really foremost, that all rowers should be treated as unique, individual human beings, and that their identity extends far beyond their disability.

REFERENCES

1. Burke, C., & McDaniel, J. B. (2001). *A Special Kind of Hero: Chris Burkes Own Story.* Nebraska, USA: iUniverse.com Inc.
2. FISA classification information sheet, available on the World Rowing website at:http://www.worldrowing.com/mm/Document/General/General/12/68/56/FISAClassificationInformationSheet_Neutral.pdf
3. Paulson, T., & Goosey-Tolfrey, V. (2018). Applying Strength and Conditioning Practices to Athletes with a Disability. In Turner, A. (ed.) *Routledge Handbook of Strength and Conditioning: Sport-specific programming for high performance.* Routledge, pp. 38–48.
4. Lennon, N., Thorpe, D., Balemans, A., Fragala-Pinkham, M., O'Neil, M., Bjornson, K., Boyd, R., & Dallmeijer, A. (2015). The Clinimetric Properties of Aerobic and Anaerobic Fitness Measures in Adults with Cerebral Palsy: A systematic review of the literature. *Research in Developmental Disabilities*. 45–6. 316–28.

11 COMMON INJURIES WITHIN ROWING

An injury is not a process of recovery, it's a process of discovery

Conor McGregor[1]

COMMON INJURIES AND THEIR POTENTIAL CAUSES

Chapter 3 has already identified that rowing is a whole body movement. Rowers will transfer load from the foot stretch, through the legs, trunk and arms and onto the oar handle. This will result in boat propulsion. With the evidence demonstrating the demand across the trunk during the drive phase[2], there are more common sites of injury and types of injury that rowers will be exposed to. The areas most commonly affected by injury are the chest wall, ribs and the spine. The lumbar spine seems to be the most common site of spinal injury, both from the evidence and through personal experience of reducing injury occurrence and rehabbing rowers back to full health. The evidence would also suggest that male rowers suffer from greater lumbar spine injuries, while female rowers suffer with a high incidence of chest wall injuries.[3]

LOW BACK

To understand how some of these injuries may occur, it is useful to explore some of the mechanical demands of rowing in a little more detail along with additional factors that may contribute to this. Understanding the drive phase is important as it is the point at which the boat hull is moving at its slowest and where the rower will start to apply force to accelerate the boat hull. This is movement where the rower will also be placed under the greatest internal and external loading during the entire rowing stroke.[4] The drive phase starts once the blade of the oar enters the water (the catch) when the rower is in a fully compressed position to the point at which the blades leave the water (finish) when the rower is in an open and extended position.[5] Rowers will go through a large back extension movement during the drive phase of the rowing stroke.[6] This will contribute to around one-third of the rowing stroke power.[7] Recent evidence from a colleague, Erica Buckeridge, demonstrated that the load across the lower back increases with incremental changes in training intensity.[8] As the rower increases the intensity of rowing either through increased rate or force per stroke, they will increase the

COMMON INJURIES WITHIN ROWING

Fig. 11.1 The catch.

Fig. 11.2 End of drive phase.

load the lumbar spine is exposed to. This can explain in part why there is a high rate of reported lumbar spine injuries.[9]

Rowers who suffer from back pain have been found to have an increase in back musculature.[10] This increase however is not fully understood in terms of whether this is as a result of the back pain or causative of it. There is evidence to suggest the increase in muscle mass is a result of an altered lumbopelvic rhythm from back pain.[11] One investigation studying elite lightweight and female rowers discovered a large variation in the left-right foot force asymmetries.[12] While the exact cause and mechanism to these asymmetries is unclear, the impact is a potential increase in asymmetrical loading through the lumbopelvic region, resulting in an increased risk of low back pain, dysfunction and injury.

During the rowing stroke, rowers may experience high spinal flexion and compression forces with sweep rowers having higher rotational forces.[13] Asymmetrical patterns have been observed between the left and right erector spinae muscle groups during flexion of sweep rowers. This is significantly related

COMMON INJURIES WITHIN ROWING

Fig. 11.5 Hip thrusts – start/finish position.

Fig. 11.6 Hip thrusts – top of ascent.

Chapter 13 for more detail on performing these exercises) to develop high-force capabilities of the hamstring complex. However, due to the nature of the rowing stroke during the end of the drive phase (Fig. 11.2), rowers will tend to bias the loading of these hip hinge movements through the lumbar and thoracic spine musculature, which are more mechanically advantaged to do so than the hamstring complex during this forward pitch movement. The lumbar and thoracic spine musculature of rowers tend to have a greater maximal force capacity than normal populations due to the extension component of the drive phase of the rowing stroke (Figs 11.1 and 11.2).[27] This greater maximal force capacity may preferentially bias loading the spinal musculature over the hamstring complex and posterior hip during this type of hip hinge movement. To overcome this, the inclusion of more knee-dominant hamstring exercises has been used. Knee dominant hamstring exercises have been found to better target the maximal force and work capacity capabilities. Exercises include machine-based hamstring curls and suspension straps hamstring curls (Figs 11.3 and 11.4). Initially, the bias of hamstring-based exercises should focus on the knee dominant exercises. When the rower's high-force and work capacity is increased, straight-legged exercises can be reintroduced. Posterior hip dominant exercises such as hip thrusts (Figs 11.5 and 11.6) would also be recommended to be included throughout.

CHEST WALL

One mechanism for rib injury is rib cage compression model. This is where peak handle force, the timing of peak neuromuscular activity of the chest-wall musculature and the thoracic muscles' high isometric force occur at similar timings, creating a ring of compression around the rib cage.[28] Activities such as rowing are susceptible to the rib cage compression model and can place very large forces across the rib cage, which can be a risk for novice rowers, those with previous injury history or those under fatigue. The bench pull is a common exercise within a rowing strength-training programme. Based on the rib cage compression model and with a rower lying prone (lying down facing the floor) on the bench while completing the exercise, it is possible this will amplify the compression of the rib cage. While the intention of the bench pull is to be preservative to rib chest wall health, it may in fact increase the risk of injury. This is not suggesting the bench pull should be removed from training programmes, but suggesting cautionary use to help mitigate against an avoidable injury. This is especially true for rowers who are returning from rib and chest wall pain and injuries. Grading a rower's return to this type of loading is necessary. While most pulling exercises will have an inherent risk, alternatives such as the seated row may be a more suitable way to load the rower.

As an addition to loading the chest wall, the use of pullovers has been introduced (Figs 11.7 and 11.8). This initially stemmed from rowers struggling to lift overhead without hyper-extending the thoracic spine. However, when a rower is in a supine position (lying down facing the ceiling), they can safely load the chest wall musculature. Chapter 9, which focuses on work capacity, provides greater insight into the programming of such exercises to increase the load tolerance of this area.

Lightweight Rowers

It is important to highlight this subgroup of rowers. Lightweight rowers have a specific risk factor around rib and chest wall injury. Due to the weight restrictions for lightweight rowers and the attempt to maintain a bodyweight close to competition weight, some lightweight rowers may be in continual calorie deficit,

COMMON INJURIES WITHIN ROWING

Fig. 11.7 Pullover – start/finish position.

Fig. 11.8 Pullover – end of descent.

which will place added physical demands on them. The restriction of calories can negatively affect bone mineral density, due to testosterone levels being decreased.[29] Testosterone levels of endurance athletes have previously been shown to be supressed[30], while these additional areas place lightweight rowers at a potentially greater risk of injury.[31] To manage this risk, it is advised that all rowers, but specifically lightweight rowers, are continually monitored for health and well-being to ensure early detection of any abnormality and appropriate action taken.

HIP

There has been an increase in reported anterior hip pain which may be due to femoral acetabular impingement (FAI), that has also resulted in increases in labral tears[32] – this has only started to be properly diagnosed through recent advances in imaging while scanning the hip.[33] The mechanism for this type of impingement is similar to that of the low back. The hip is placed into a deep flexion position (see Fig. 11.1). In this position, the hip is not only in deep flexion but is starting to internally rotate. This reduces the space for the head of the femur to move freely in the acetabulum of the hip, causing the impingement.[34] This can be further exacerbated when rowers attempt to complete the catch position but may have functional restrictions around ankles or spine resulting in the hip having to anteriorly rotate to a greater degree. This further reduces the space for the head of the femur to move within the acetabulum. This can increase the risk of the impingement further. Management of this can include ensuring the ankle has adequate dorsi-flexion range of movement and that the foot stretcher set-up in the boat or on the ergometer allows full functional range of the ankle. If there is a range of movement deficits around the spine, the inclusion of mobility exercises to increase or maintain normal range of movement becomes important.

Capacity and maximal force expression capabilities of the adductor group can also be supportive in managing the risk of impingement. With the adductors being the prime hip extensors when the hip is in 90 degree or greater flexion, it may have the ability to maintain the hip position during the catch phase. This may allow the maintenance of a near normal head of femur within the acetabulum without a significant reduction in space for the head to move in. Adductor-based exercises can include isometrically squeezing a medicine ball between the knees for short maximal durations of up to 10 seconds, accumulating 60 seconds of work within a set (10 seconds recovery between each squeeze) and repeat for three sets. Adjusting the hip position while performing this exercise (lying on back with feet on floor so hip is around 120 degrees or lying on back with feet off floor with knees above hips so hip is at 90 degrees) can vary this exercise. Alternatively using the hip adductor machine in most fitness gyms is a good alternative.

KNEE

While knee pain may be common in rowers, it tends not to be traumatic ligamentous or meniscal damage.[35] The most common experience is likely to be generalized patella-femoral pain syndrome or tendinopathy. These are known to cause lateral knee pain if not effectively treated.[36] The rowing stroke requires the knee to go through a very large range of movement from the catch to the end of the drive phase[37,38] (see Figs 11.1 and 11.2). This places the knee in deep flexion, where it is subjected to high compression forces which can result in excessive wear on the hyaline cartilage of the under-surface of the patella.[39] This can result in the generalized patella-femoral pain syndrome.[40] The low back section within this chapter articulates some of the mechanical reasoning for pain and injury which is similar to that of the knee. When the hip, trunk and spine are not functioning appropriately, there is a chance that the resulting dysfunction carries across to joints above and below the affected area. In this case, the knee pain experienced by some rowers may be as a result of the low back dysfunction by increasing the compressive forces around the knee, increased range of movement expected through the knee and potentially malalignment of knee tracking during flexion and extension tasks.[41] These could all result in progressively more degenerative knee pain if not corrected early.[42,43] While the development of work capacity and maximal force expression around the knee extensors and flexors can alleviate some or all of the pain, it does not remove some of the potential causes.[44] Focusing attention around the posterior hip as described in the low back section of this chapter may potentially remove the cause of the pain.[45,46]

CONCLUSION

This chapter attempts to highlight the common injuries based on the literature and experiences with working rowers. This is not an exhaustive list as there are many other injuries and dysfunctions rowers can and will experience. For a greater review and in-depth discussion around injuries, the Thornton *et al.* (2016) article is an excellent resource to refer to.[47]

It is also pertinent to state that the largest risk factor in the majority of rowing-related injuries is the rapid increase in training intensity, volume or frequency.[48] This is a risk factor that can be accounted for and managed. To do this effectively, having a single training programme for each rower that encompasses all training regardless of type is necessary. This can only be achieved when the entire performance support team (coaches and practitioners) are working together to an aligned training purpose. A high-level view can then be taken to explore the potential risk factors of rapid spikes of training intensity, volume or frequency.

REFERENCES

1. Conor McGregor Quotes. (n.d.). AZquotes.com. Retrieved November 8, 2019, from AZquotes.com Website: www.azquotes.com/quote/1064103
2. Klesnev, V. (1991). Improvement of dynamical structure of the drive in rowing. PhD Thesis. Saint-Petersburg Institute of Sport.
3. Hickery, G. J., Fricker, P. A., & McDonald, W. A. (1997). Injuries to Elite Rowers over a 10-year Period. *Medicine and Science in Sports & Exercise.* 29, 1,567–72.
4. Thompson, P., & Wolf, A. (2015). *Training for the Complete Rower: A guide to improving your performance.* Wiltshire, UK: The Crowood Press.
5. *Ibid.*
6. Secher, N. H. (1993). Physiological and Biomechanical Aspects of Rowing: Implications for training. *Sports Medicine.* 15, 24–42.
7. Klesnev (1991).
8. Buckeridge, E., Hislop, S., Bull, A., & McGregor, A. (2012). Kinematic Asymmetries of the Lower Limbs During Ergometer Rowing. *Medicine and Science in Sport and Exercise.* 44, 2,147–53.
9. *Ibid.*
10. McGregor, A. H., Anderton, L., & Gedroyc, W. M. W. (2002). The Trunk Muscles of Elite Oarsmen. *British Journal of Sports Medicine.* 36, 214–17.
11. Lee, J. H., Hoshino, Y., Nakamura, K., Kariya, Y., Saita, K., & Ito, K. (1999). Trunk Muscle Weakness as a Risk Factor for Low Back Pain. *Spine.* 24, 54–7.

12. Buckeridge, E. M., Bull, A. M., & McGregor, A. H. (2014). Foot Force Production and Asymmetries in Elite Rowers. *Sports Biomechanics*. 13, 47–61.
13. Adams, M., & Dolan, P. (1995). Recent Advances in the Lumbar Spine Mechanics and their Clinical Significance. *Clinical Biomechanics*. 10, 13–19.
14. Parkin, S., Norwicky, A. L., Rutherford, O. M., & McGregor, A. H. (2001). Do Oarsmen have Asymmetries in the Strength of their Back and Leg Muscles? *Journal of Sports Science*. 19, 521–26.
15. Gajdosik, R., Hatcher, C., & Whitesell, S. (1992). Influence of Short Hamstring Muscles on the Pelvis and Lumbar Spine in Standing and During the Toe Touch Test. *Clinical Biomechanics*. 7, 38–42.
16. *Ibid.*
17. *Ibid.*
18. Buckeridge *et al.* (2014).
19. Buckeridge *et al.* (2012).
20. Gajdosik *et al.* (1992).
21. McGregor *et al.* (2002).
22. Spencer, S., Wolf, A., & Rushton, A. (2016). Spinal-Exercise Prescription in Sport: Classifying physical training and rehabilitation by intention and outcome. *Journal of Athletic Training*. 51, 613–28.
23. Gajdosik *et al.* (1992).
24. Adams & Dolan (1995).
25. Gajdosik *et al.* (1992).
26. *Ibid.*
27. Secher (1993).
28. Vinthers, A. (2008). Rib Stress Fractures in Elite Rowers, Lund University, Lund, Denmark.
29. Talbott, S. M., & Shapses, S. A. (1998). Fasting and Energy Intake Influence Bone Turnover in Lightweight Male Rowers. International *Journal of Sports Nutrition*. 8, 377–87.
30. Hackney, A. C. (2001). Endurance Exercise Training and Reproductive Dysfunction in Men: Alterations of the hypothalamic–pituitary–testicular axis. *Current Pharmaceutical Design*. 7, 261–73.
31. Vinthers, A., Kanstrup, I. L., Christiansen, E., Ekdal C., & Aagaard, P. (2008). Testosterone and BMD in Elite Male Lightweight Rowers. *International Journal of Sports Medicine*. 29, 803–07.
32. Wilson, F., Gissane, C., Gormley, J., & Simms, C. (2010). A 12-month Prospective Cohort Study of Injury in International Rowers. *British Journal of Sports Medicine*. 44, 207–14.
33. Boykin, R. E., McFeely, E. D., Ackerman, K. E., Yen, Y. M., Nasreddine, A., & Kocher, M. S. (2013). Labral Injuries of the Hip in Rowers. *Clinical Orthopaedics and Related Research*. 471, 2,517–22.
34. *Ibid.*
35. Waryasz, G., & McDermott, A. (2008). Patellofemoral Pain Syndrome (PFPS): A systematic review of anatomy and potential risk factors. *Dynamic Medicine*. 7:9.
36. Thornton, J. S., Vinther, A., Wilson, F., Lebrun, C. M., Wilkinson, M., Di Ciacca, S. R., Orlando, K., & Smoljanovic, T. (2016). Rowing Injuries: An updated review. Sports Medicine. 47, 641–61.
37. Waryasz & McDermott (2008).
38. Wilson *et al.* (2010).
39. *Ibid.*
40. Waryasz & McDermott (2008).
41. Wilson *et al.* (2010).
42. Waryasz & McDermott (2008).
43. Wilson *et al.* (2010).
44. *Ibid.*
45. Waryasz & McDermott (2008).
46. Wilson *et al.* (2010).
47. Thornton *et al.* (2016).
48. *Ibid.*

12 | TRANSFER OF TRAINING

Our potential lies between what is and what could be

Kim Butler[1]

INTRODUCTION

The previous chapters have shared insights and experiences of constructing S&C programmes to support the coach's model of performance, creating an environment for rowers to flourish and to optimize the required adaptive response. The final bit is how can S&C coaches support a greater transfer of training to the event itself? Throughout the book, the statement that S&C is not the event itself has been used. This may feel a little challenging as it is easy to judge performances in the weight room and more difficult to judge against the event or part of the event. This chapter bridges this gap to illustrate how S&C coaches can have direct impact on rowing performances, particularly when the rowing coach tends to prescribe boat, ergometer and cross training modalities.

Chapter 3 describes the demands of rowing, including where S&C may have the greatest impact within a race. The start of the race is where S&C can impact the race directly. The highest forces are recorded within the first 10 strokes[2] which has a clear link to maximal force expression. Chapter 5 articulates the idea that training methods not only need to develop physical qualities, but must be coordinatively similar to the event task itself. While training maximal force or rate of force development qualities can develop these further, the exercises themselves are not coordinatively similar to the tasks in the event. Therefore, the rower may have increased the potential to display these force characteristics and will have demonstrated them within the exercises or tasks prescribed to develop them, but not within rowing-specific movement tasks.

An opportunity exists to provide rowers with the means to transfer these physical characteristics to realize the full potential within movement tasks coordinatively similar to rowing. The use of ergometers and the rowing boat for short explosive tasks provides this opportunity for rowers to fully express the newly developed physical qualities within rowing-specific tasks.

SHORT ERGOMETER SPRINTS

Using the rowing ergometer is probably the

TRANSFER OF TRAINING

easiest way for rowers to transfer the newly developed force characteristics. While the ergometer is not water-based and remains in a stable platform, it does provide the opportunity for rowers to apply forces in a very similar pattern to the rowing stroke in a boat. As long as rowers maintain full distance per stroke, the rower will still move themselves into the correct positions using correct technique (rockover into the catch position and maintain correct body positioning within the drive and recovery phases).

There are several varying methods rowers can use to support this transfer of training. This ranges from 3–10 power strokes, 100m and 30-second maximal efforts on the ergometer. Having prescribed all of these in some capacity previously, the preferred method is using power strokes; 7–10 power strokes generally allow the rower to perform maximally without having to work for extended periods. The power strokes are the easiest to administer and can get many rowers completing simultaneously. Power strokes also seem to have the least fatigue burden on the rower post-completion and most rowers are capable of doing several efforts within a single strength-training session as part of a standard training day. Across all the methods identified above, the rowers worked with seem to find power strokes the preferred option. The advantage of using the ergometers is data can be collected per stroke and overall performance within the effort. When comparing the data across the methods, there is little difference between them: the ergometers are reliable and therefore provide consistent information about each rower. Mean power is the most useful metric to record and not split for 500m, which is the most common metric on Concept2 ergometers. Split times span a range of mean power values so are not accurate enough to use. Recording mean power provides some evidence of the transfer of training. Mean power scores will increase as rowers become more adept at applying the force characteristics during the rowing stroke. Because of the diversity of methods, it is difficult to provide standards for different rowing categories. It is advised to collate data on the rowers worked with and establish standards specific to that population of rowers.

Power Stroke Set-up: 7–10 Strokes

1. Rowers should warm up thoroughly and include short maximal efforts on the ergometer prior to completing the efforts.
2. Rowers will be working maximally so it is advised to fix the ergometer in place to avoid it moving during the effort.
3. Rowers should set the drag of the ergometer to the normal setting.
4. Rowers should fix feet on the foot stretcher to allow full range of movement around the first metatarsal (big toe).
5. Rowers can either start from a stationary or moving flywheel. A stationary flywheel will be similar to that of the first stroke at the start of the race. A moving flywheel will be similar to increasing stroke rate and boat speed from a lower stroke rate and speed.
6. Rowers can either self-start or the start can be initiated by a coach if many rowers are completing simultaneously.
7. Rowers can be prescribed a specific stroke rate or be allowed to self-select a stroke rate.
8. Rowers are required to maintain full stroke length throughout the effort.
9. Once rowers have completed the 7–10 strokes, the mean power score is recorded. It is beneficial to have several personnel to observe and help collate the data from the computer unit of the ergometer.

Rowers can complete between 3–6 efforts of 7–10 power strokes with 3–4 minutes recovery between each of them. Based on this prescription method, this allows power strokes to be easily included within a traditional S&C

programme. It is best to complete after the warm-up at the start of the session to allow the rowers the best opportunity to transfer the force characteristics. Interestingly, drag does not influence power per stroke but stroke rate does. Rowers will always have a decline in power per stroke as stroke rate increases. However, the rowers who have the highest power per stroke at lower rates (20–24 strokes per minute) have the smallest decay in power per stroke as the rate increases to above 50 strokes per minute when compared to rowers with lower power per stroke at the same rates. This suggests rowers with the smallest decay as rate increases are potentially able to make big boats and small boats move more quickly than rowers with larger decay as rates increase (and therefore lower absolute power per stroke across stroke rates).

WATER SPRINTS

Prior to working with rowing, I spent several years working with track and field athletes. There was one sprinter who was preparing for an Olympic Games. The coach of this sprinter came to find me to say that the athlete needed specific training to help with their start. The coach went on to say the athlete's start was not very good and would be the one thing that would make the biggest difference. The coach asked for specific exercises to be completed in the weight room to help the start, which the athlete also wanted. To get a better understanding of the coach and athlete's need, all training sessions were attended and observed. Within the first session, the decision was made to record the number of starts practised. At the end of the week, the accumulated start practices were shared with the coach and athlete. The athlete had practised less than five times at maximal effort. The answer to improving start performance was not in the gym but on the track, where the coach adopted the new insight and changed the programme to include more starts. The athlete went on to become number one in the British all-time rankings.

The story is shared as it provides a good example of what has also been observed in rowing. For rowers to be able to appropriately transfer training qualities into performances, there need to be enough opportunities to do so. Rowing coaches will tend to prescribe and coach all the on-water training so there is a need to work closely with coaches to be able to provide appropriate opportunities. High-intensity, short water-sprints are not commonplace, particularly outside of the competition period. This places a large burden on the small number of opportunities that exist during competition phases to effectively transfer any of the training qualities to the boat. Unlike ergometer power strokes, water sprints are a lot more challenging to prescribe within a strength-training session! That said, it is possible for rowers to have regular exposure to water sprints by planning and coordinating their use in the same way all training is planned throughout the season. This does require working closely with the coaching staff to make time available within existing on-water training sessions.

Water Sprint Set-up

Like ergometer power strokes, water sprints can be performed from a stationary position or from a moving position. Stationary can replicate the start while moving can replicate changes in rate and speed as experienced within racing itself. Rather than number of strokes or specific stroke rates, distance tends to work more effectively on the water. This is mostly due to the racing demands being over the distance which rowers are more comfortable with. Usually 100m from a stationary or moving start is preferred but any distance up to 250m can be completed. Most boats now have some computer interface providing feedback around speed, distance and split rate. Any of these metrics are fine to record to keep track of changes. Alternatively, having a distance marked out with a coach on the bank or launch boat to record the time from a stopwatch is equally effective.

CONCLUSION

Transfer of training for rowers does not need to be complicated. Using the existing methods of training and manipulating them as required is a simple way to support the transfer of training characteristics into performances. This type of training can be viewed as training load within an S&C programme, either within a session or supplementary to ergometer and water-based training. For this to be feasible though, there must be close collaboration with the rowing coaches to be able to fit all the training together as a single plan.

REFERENCES

1. Butler, K. D. (1998). *Freedoms Given, Freedoms Won: Afro-Brazilians in Post-Abolition São Paolo and Salvador.* New Jersey, USA: Rutgers University Press.
2. Hartman, U., Mader, A., Wasser, K., & Klauer, I. (1993). Peak Force, Velocity, and Power During Five and Ten Maximal Rowing Ergometer Strokes by World Class Female and Male Rowers. *International Journal of Sports Medicine.* 14 (Suppl. 1), S42–S45.

13 EXERCISE TECHNIQUE

Jack Birch

Master technique and then forget about it and be natural

Anna Pavlova[1]

INTRODUCTION

Rowing, and any other sport for that matter, has unique demands (*see* Chapter 3) and thus athletes will naturally adopt and develop their own movement identities within the sport and weight room. A sound understanding of the sport will give you an insight into these movement identities and will enable you to better bridge the gap between requirements of the sport, the athlete and how the weight room can support both of those elements. Once an understanding of the sport has been developed, we can begin to understand what is important in the sport and understand why our athletes adopt certain movement characteristics, how specific exercises will support physical development within the sport and also how we can mitigate injury risk outside and inside of the weight room.

A primary tool in any S&C coach's toolbox is an ability to understand technical models of key exercise techniques typically implemented in their sport, alongside an understanding of how to coach and correct these techniques. There are many excellent comprehensive resources in current literature which can provide coaches with information pertaining to current standard resistance training techniques alongside their variations.[2] Although a strong understanding of the technical models of standard exercises is fundamental and will support your practice, in the real world, when we are coaching, what we see in front of us rarely reflects what we see in the textbook.

When observing an athlete complete an exercise repetition, in 99 out of 100 cases, it will not completely reflect the perfect technical model. Take a squat for example in a novice lifter; the bar is on the back; observations would suggest similarities in the movement pattern around the hip and knee joints. However, the coach can detect that the movement patterns are different and do not seem optimal. So, in this huge majority of cases, when the movement doesn't match the model, what does the coach do? This chapter will aim to in part answer that question by providing an insight into some of the exercises we use to support rowing athletes, alongside how they are coached to optimize individual techniques and performance. This chapter is by no means an exhaustive list. However, it should be used

EXERCISE TECHNIQUE

as a reference to provide an understanding of our current practices, alongside some of the common themes often observed within rowing populations.

BACK SQUAT

Exercise Objective

The back squat is the primary lower-body strength exercise used within rowing to develop strength qualities around the hips and knees. The key muscle groups that the back squat utilizes are the quadriceps, gluteals and hamstrings.

Relation to Rowing

The back squat supports the rowing stroke as it can develop the strength qualities in the lower body and trunk to support a powerful drive phase from the catch position. In addition, a full-range deep back squat mimics the catch position at the front of the stroke and enables the rower to be strong and stable at the start of the drive phase. To further understand the leg drive position please refer to Chapter 2 in *Training for the Complete Rower: A guide to improving your performance.*[3]

Gym Hygiene
- Understanding how to squat safely with and without spotters is essential, including how to fail a lift safely.
- Pay careful attention to how each squat rack can be adjusted to de-rack and rack the bar safely and effectively and how to adjust the safety bars to the correct height for the depth of the squat.
- Ensure the lifting area is free from obstacles, such as unused weight plates and gym equipment.

Set-Up
- Set the bar to the height of the armpit of the athlete.
- Stand at arm's length away from the bar, taking a comfortable grip slightly outside of the shoulders – use the markings on the bar to ensure symmetry of hand position.
- Step under the centre of the bar with feet directly under the bar.
- Create a 'shelf' for the bar to rest on by drawing back the shoulder blades.
- The bar should rest on the fleshy 'shelf' and not the bony protrusions of the neck. Athletes should maintain this position throughout the lift.
- Before de-racking the bar, the athlete should pull the shoulder blades together, elevate the chest and keep their head and spine neutral.
- Take a deep breath and hold.
- Lift the bar from the rack and take a small step backwards to clear the rack.
- Adjust feet to between hip and slightly greater than shoulder width with toes pointing at 11 (left) and 1 (right) on the clock face – each athlete will have a slightly different set-up which optimizes their squat performance.
- Weight distribution should be mid-foot in the starting position.

Fig. 13.1 Back squat – start/finish position.

EXERCISE TECHNIQUE

Descent
- Ensure the shoulder blades are drawn backwards and downwards, maintaining a neutral spine and head position. Take a deep breath in to increase intra-abdominal pressure and maintain a neutral spine throughout the movement.
- Under control, simultaneously flex the hips and knees so that the hips move backwards past the heels of the feet. Correct squat depth is when the femur of the athlete reaches parallel to the floor.
- The spine should be in a neutral position with no rounding of the upper back (thoracic spine) or flattening of the low back (lumbar spine). The normal curvature of the spine should be maintained throughout the lift.
- The weight distribution will move from mid-foot to heel during the descent.
- The hip, knee and ankle alignment should be maintained throughout and knees should track the line of the feet.
- The angle of the trunk and shin in relation to the floor should be fairly similar to each other.

Transition Phase
- In this phase, downward movement ceases and upward movement is initiated.
- This phase should take place when the mid-thigh (the femur) is at least parallel to the floor.
- The angle of the trunk and shin should be similar.
- When the athlete reaches this position, they should then initiate the drive out of the squat and use the elastic components of the muscles and connective tissues to assist the concentric action of the squat to overcome the load.

Ascent
- This phase is initiated via triple extension of the hip, knee and ankle.
- The athlete should aggressively return the bar to the start by forcibly driving the heels into the floor.
- The hips and shoulders should rise simultaneously at the same speed with the spine maintaining its neutral position.
- The weight distribution should move from heel to mid-foot towards the top of the ascent.
- Exhale from previous deep breath and inhale again in preparation for the next repetition.

Re-Racking
- Walk forward into the rack until hearing both the left and right side make contact with the rack.
- Squat the bar back into the rack – don't lean forward to rack the bar as this can increase the risk of injury.

Corrective Exercise: Box Squat

Gym Hygiene
- Understanding how to squat safely with and without spotters is essential, including how to fail a lift safely.
- Pay careful attention to how each squat rack can be adjusted to de-rack and rack the bar safely and effectively and how to

Fig. 13.2 Back squat – end of descent position.

EXERCISE TECHNIQUE

Table 13.1 Back squat common faults

Common Fault	Technical Points	Coaching Points	Corrective Exercises
Hips rise first during the ascent	Reduce the load	Lead with a 'big chest'	Front Squat (see Front Squat technical model)
	Is the athlete leaning forward too much?	Stand up	Quadriceps Strength Exercises: Front Squat, Leg Press, Leg Extension
	Hips and chest rise at same rate	Drive through the heels	Ankle Mobility: Focus on gastrocnemius/soleus complex
	Increase glute activation through hip abduction	Turn toes out	
	Initiate the ascent by driving heels into the floor		
Knee valgus (Knees coming together)	Reduce the load	Drive the knees outwards away from each other	Single Leg Counterbalanced Squats
	Is it unilateral or bilateral?	Adjust width of the feet and toes position to support knee alignment	Banded Squats (Band around knees)
	Is there a compensation at the ankle?	Screw the feet into the floor and tear it apart. Imagine trying to tear newspaper apart with your feet on the floor	Abductor Strength Exercises: Monster walks, cable abduction, seated hip abductions
Depth	Reduce the load	Widen the stance position	Box Squat (see Box Squat technical model)
	Check stance width and angle	Turn the toes out	Ankle Mobility: Dorsiflexion and Plantar Flexion
	Is the ankle mobility a limiting factor?	Push knees out	Hip Mobility: Extensor and Flexor Mobility
	Is hip mobility a limiting factor?		
Flexed spine during the descent and/or ascent	Reduce the load	Big chest	Front Squat (see Front Squat technical model)
	Maintain neutral lumbar spine	Instruct rower to 'squeeze a £20 note between their shoulder blades'	Goblet Squat
	Maintain normal thoracic extension	Brace trunk throughout the lift	Good Mornings
	Scapula set back and down		Back Strength Exercises: Good Mornings, Bench Pull (see Bench Pull technical model), Seated Row, Pull Up
			Anterior Trunk Strength Exercises: Barbell Rollouts, Eleknas
			Lumbo-Pelvic Dissociation Exercises: Bird Dogs, Deadbugs

EXERCISE TECHNIQUE

Fig. 13.3 Box squat – start/finish position.

EXERCISE TECHNIQUE

adjust the safety bars to the correct height for the depth of the squat.
- Ensure the lifting area is free from obstacles such as unused weight plates and gym equipment.

Set-Up
- Ensure box is strong and stable enough to take significant load and large enough for athlete to make contact with box. Box must be set up to a height whereby the rower's mid-thigh (when seated) is parallel to the floor. Box must be set up behind the lifting position. Test this position out with an unloaded bar to ensure appropriate set-up.
- Set the bar to the height of the armpit of the athlete.
- Stand at arm's length away from the bar, taking a comfortable grip slightly outside of the shoulders – use the markings on the bar to ensure symmetry of hand position.
- Step under the centre of the bar with feet directly under the bar.
- Create a 'shelf' for the bar to rest on by drawing back the shoulder blades.
- The bar should rest on the fleshy 'shelf' and not the bony protrusions of the neck. Athlete should maintain this position throughout the lift.
- Before de-racking the bar, the athlete should pull the shoulder blades together, elevate the chest and keep their head and spine neutral.
- Take a deep breath and hold.
- Lift the bar from the rack and take a small step backwards to clear the rack.
- Athlete should move feet to slightly greater width than they would for a typical back squat set-up (*see* back squat technical model, Figs 13.1 and 13.2) with toes pointing at 11 (left) and 1 (right) on the clock face – each rower will have a slightly different set-up which optimizes their squat performance.
- Weight distribution should be mid-foot in the starting position.

Descent
- Ensure the shoulder blades are drawn backwards and downwards, maintaining a neutral spine and head position. Take a deep breath in to increase intra-abdominal pressure and maintain a neutral spine throughout the movement.
- Under control, simultaneously flex the hips and knees so that the hips move backwards past the heels of the feet. Correct squat depth is when the femur of the athlete reaches parallel to the floor.
- The spine should be in a neutral position with no rounding of the upper back (thoracic spine) or flattening of the low back (lumbar spine). The normal curvature of the spine should be maintained throughout the lift.
- The weight distribution will move from mid-foot to heel during the descent.
- The hip, knee and ankle alignment should be maintained throughout and knees should track the line of the feet.
- The angle of the trunk and shin in relation to the floor should be fairly similar to each other.

Static/Relaxed Phase
- In this phase, downward movement ceases and the athlete should briefly sit down on the box in a controlled manner (not rocking on, dropping onto, bouncing off or completing a touch-and-go on the box).
- This phase should take place when the mid-thigh (the femur) is at least parallel to the floor.
- The angle of the trunk and shin in relation to the floor should remain similar.
- When the athlete reaches the box, they should briefly pause and then initiate an aggressive drive out of the bottom of the squat.

Ascent
- This phase is initiated via triple extension of the hip, knee and ankle.

125

EXERCISE TECHNIQUE

Fig. 13.4 Box squat – end of descent position.

EXERCISE TECHNIQUE

- The athlete should aggressively return the bar to the start by forcibly driving the heels into the floor.
- The hips and shoulders should rise simultaneously at the same speed with the spine maintaining its neutral position.
- The weight distribution should move from heel to mid-foot towards the top of the ascent.
- Exhale from previous deep breath and inhale again in preparation for the next repetition.

Re-Racking
- Walk forward into the rack until hearing both the left and right side make contact with the rack.
- Squat the bar back into the rack – don't lean forward to rack the bar as this can increase the risk of injury.

Corrective Exercise: Front Squat

Gym Hygiene
- Understanding how to squat safely with and without spotters is essential, including how to fail a lift safely.
- Pay careful attention to how each squat rack can be adjusted to de-rack and rack the bar safely and effectively and how to adjust the safety bars to the correct height for the depth of the squat.
- Ensure the lifting area is free from obstacles such as unused weight plates and gym equipment.

Set-Up
- Set the bar to the height of the armpit of the athlete.
- Stand at arm's length away from the bar, taking a comfortable grip slightly outside of the shoulders. Use the markings on the bar to ensure symmetry of hand position.

Fig. 13.5 Front squat – start/finish position.

- Step under the centre of the bar with feet directly under the bar.
- Create a 'shelf' for the bar to rest on by pulling the elbows underneath the bar and placing it on top of the anterior deltoids and clavicles.
- The elbows should be fully flexed in a position where the upper arms are parallel to the floor. This is the optimal front rack position.
- Before de-racking the bar, the athlete should ensure elbows are pulled under the bar and upper arms are parallel to the floor, then elevate the chest and keep their head and spine in a neutral position.
- Take a deep breath and hold.
- Lift the bar from the rack and take a small step backwards to clear the rack.
- Adjust feet to between hip and slightly greater than shoulder width with toes pointing at 11 (left) and 1 (right) on the clock face – each athlete will have a slightly different set-up which optimizes their squat performance.
- Weight distribution should be mid-foot in the starting position.

127

EXERCISE TECHNIQUE

Descent
- Ensure the elbows are high, chest is up and out with the head in a neutral position. Take a deep breath in to increase intra-abdominal pressure and maintain a neutral spine throughout the movement.
- Under control, simultaneously flex the hips and knees so that the hips move backwards past the heels of the feet. Correct squat depth is when the femur is parallel with the floor.
- The spine should be in a neutral position with no rounding of the upper back (thoracic spine) or flattening of the low back (lumbar spine). The normal curvature of the spine should be maintained throughout the lift.
- The weight distribution will move from mid-foot to heels during the descent.
- The hip, knee and ankle alignment should be maintained throughout and knees should track the line of the feet.
- The angle of the trunk and shin in relation to the floor should be fairly similar.

Transition Phase
- In this phase, downward movement ceases and upward movement is initiated.
- This phase should take place when the mid-thigh (the femur) is at least parallel to the floor.
- The angle of the trunk and shin should be similar.
- When the athlete reaches this position, they should then initiate the drive out of the squat and use the elastic components of the muscles and connective tissues, to assist the concentric action of the squat to overcome the load.

Ascent
- This phase is initiated via triple extension of the hip, knee and ankle.
- The athlete should aggressively return the bar to the start by forcibly driving the heels into the floor.
- The hips and shoulders should rise simultaneously at the same speed with the spine maintaining its neutral position.
- The weight distribution should move from heel to mid-foot towards the top of the ascent.
- Exhale from previous deep breath and inhale again in preparation for the next repetition.

Re-Racking
- Walk forward into the rack until hearing both the left and right side make contact with the rack.
- Squat the bar back into the rack – don't lean forward to rack the bar as this can increase the risk of injury.

DEADLIFT

Exercise Objective

The deadlift is a key strength exercise used in rowing. The deadlift will predominantly develop strength qualities around the hips, knees and back. The primary muscles that the deadlift utilizes are the gluteals, quadriceps, hamstrings, adductor magnus and erector spinae.

Relation to Rowing

The deadlift supports the rowing stroke as it can develop the strength qualities in the lower body, trunk and back to support a powerful drive phase from the catch position. It encourages a movement pattern that mimics and overloads the drive phase of the stroke.

Gym Hygiene
- Understand how to fail safely as there is no need for spotters.
- Ensure the lifting area is free from obstacles such as unused weight plates and gym equipment.

EXERCISE TECHNIQUE

Fig. 13.6 Front squat – end of descent position.

- Full-size bumper weights should be used when lifting from the floor, anything smaller in diameter will increase stress on the lower back.

Set-Up
- Step up to the bar with the bar sitting over the toes and the feet around hip-width apart – each athlete will have a slightly different set-up which optimizes their deadlift performance.
- Take an overhand grip over the bar (palms facing towards you). The grip should be just wider than the outside of your legs. Ensure the athlete has a strong grip of the bar and does not allow the bar to hang from the fingers.
- The arms should be fully extended with shoulders directly above the bar.
- The hips should be slightly higher than the knees with the back maintaining a neutral position throughout the lift.
- Take a deep breath in and hold.
- The athlete should create tension through the body by pulling slightly against the bar without the bar lifting off the floor.
- The weight distribution should be midfoot to heel.

129

EXERCISE TECHNIQUE

Ascent
- Initiate the movement by driving the feet into the floor.
- The hips and shoulders should rise simultaneously at the same speed with the spine maintaining a neutral position.
- Shoulders should remain directly above the bar until the bar passes the knees, at which point the trunk becomes more upright through an aggressive hip extension.
- The weight distribution moves from the heels to the mid-foot towards the top of the ascent.
- The bar should move in an upwards and slightly backwards direction and should always be in contact/near contact with the body.
- At the top of the ascent, exhale.

Descent
- There are physiological adaptation benefits to returning the bar to the floor for the posterior chain (gluteals and hamstrings) but only with submaximal loads. If this is a maximal lift, it is recommended to drop the bar from the top of the ascent.
- If the load is submaximal, the athlete should complete the ascent in reverse with a slight flexion from the hips first, lowering the bar to just above the knees.
- Control the bar to the floor.
- Alternatively, drop the bar from the top of the ascent.

Fig. 13.7 Deadlift – start/finish position.

EXERCISE TECHNIQUE

Fig. 13.8 Deadlift – top of the ascent position.

EXERCISE TECHNIQUE

Table 13.2 Deadlift common faults

Common Fault	Technical Points	Coaching Points	Corrective Exercises
Flexed spine	Reduce the load	Brace the trunk	Posterior Chain Strength Exercises: RDLs (see RDL technical model), Good Mornings (see Good Morning technical model), Hip Thrust (see Hip Thrust technical model)
	Ensure pre-tension on the bar at start of lift	Make a 'big chest'	Anterior Trunk Strength Exercses: Barbell Rollouts, Eleknas
	Scapula set back and down	Lead with a 'big chest'	
	Controlled speed of lift from the floor	Lift the bar smoothly from the floor	
		Take the slack out of the arms	
Hips rise first during the ascent	Reduce the load	Make a 'big chest'	Quadriceps Strength Exercises: Front Squat (see Front Squat technical model, Figs 13.5 and 13.6), Back Squat (see Back Squat technical model), Leg Press
	Ensure correct start position with hips lower than chest	Lead with a 'big chest'	Upper Back Strength Exercises: Bench Pull (see Bench Pull technical model), Pull Ups, Seated Row
	Hips and chest rise at the same rate	Drive through the heels	Anterior Trunk Strength Exercises: Barbell Rollouts, Eleknas
	Initiate the ascent by driving heels into the floor	Take the slack out of the bar	
		Sit back and down	
	Is the athlete driving through the heels or toes?	Pull the bar towards the body	Posterior Chain Strength Exercises: RDL (see RDL technical model), Good Morning (see Good Morning technical model)
	Are the athlete's hips rising early (see above common fault)?	Keep shoulder above the bar for longer	
		Drive through the heels	Hip Flexion Mobility
	Are the shoulders above the bar in the set-up position?	Lead with a 'big chest'	
		Ensure pre-tension in the bar in the setup	

EXERCISE TECHNIQUE

Corrective Exercise: Good Morning

Gym Hygiene
- Understanding how to perform a Good Morning safely is essential, including how to fail a lift safely.
- Pay careful attention to how each squat rack can be adjusted to de-rack and rack the bar safely and effectively.
- Ensure the lifting area is free from obstacles such as unused weight plates and gym equipment.

Set-Up
- Set the bar to the height of the armpit of the athlete.
- Stand at arm's length away from the bar, taking a comfortable grip slightly outside of the shoulders – use the markings on the bar to ensure symmetry of hand position.
- Step under the centre of the bar with feet directly under the bar.
- Create a 'shelf' for the bar to rest on by drawing back the shoulder blades.
- The bar should rest on the fleshy 'shelf' and not the bony protrusions of the neck. The athlete should maintain this position throughout the lift.
- Before de-racking the bar, the athlete should pull the shoulder blades together, elevate the chest and keep their head and spine neutral.
- Take a deep breath and hold.
- Lift the bar from the rack and take a small step backwards to clear the rack.
- Adjust feet to between hip and slightly greater than shoulder width with toes pointing at eleven (left) and one (right) on the clock face – each athlete will have a slightly different set-up which optimizes their squat performance.
- Weight distribution should be mid-foot in the starting position.
- The knees should be soft and slightly bent (15–20 degrees).

Fig. 13.9 Good Morning – start/finish position.

133

EXERCISE TECHNIQUE

Descent
- Initiate the movement by pushing the hips back (close a door behind you with hips) whilst maintaining a neutral spine and braced trunk.
- Ensure the shoulder blades are drawn backwards and downwards, maintaining a neutral spine and head position. Take a deep breath in to increase intra-abdominal pressure and maintain a neutral spine throughout the movement.
- The athlete should feel tension in the posterior chain throughout the descent.
- The weight distribution should shift from mid-foot to the heels.
- The bottom of the descent has been reached when either the athlete's back is parallel to the floor or the athlete's lower back begins to round. The athlete should not descend any further if the lower back is beginning to round due to injury risk at the lumbar spine.
- The knee angle (15–20 degrees) should remain constant throughout the descent.
- Bar speed should be controlled during the descent at a speed where the athlete can maintain appropriate spinal position.

Ascent
- The athlete should complete the descent in reverse, with the movement initiated from the hips and an aggressive hip extension movement, whilst maintaining a neutral spine and braced trunk.
- The athlete needs to ensure the chest is up and shoulders are drawn backwards and downwards. It is important that the extension comes from the hips and not the back.
- The weight distribution should move from heel to mid-foot during the ascent.
- Exhale from previous deep breath and inhale again in preparation for the next repetition.

Re-Racking
- Walk forward into the rack until hearing both the left and right side make contact with the rack.

Fig. 13.10 Good Morning – bottom of descent position.

EXERCISE TECHNIQUE

- Squat the bar back into the rack and don't lean forward to rack the bar, as this can increase the risk of injury.

ROMANIAN DEADLIFT (RDL)

Exercise Objective

The RDL is primarily used as a supporting strength exercise within rowing. The RDL targets similar muscles to the traditional deadlift, however it will predominantly develop strength qualities in the posterior chain, due to the slightly flexed knee position throughout the movement. The key muscles that the RDL utilizes are the hamstrings, gluteals and back.

Relation to Rowing

The RDL supports the rowing stroke as it can develop the strength qualities in muscles used during the hip extension part of the drive phase and can support efficient force transfer through the hips, as opposed to the spine during the drive phase. The RDL can also be important for developing lower-back strength to reduce injury risk in this area and also developing posterior chain strength, as rowers typically have dominant quadriceps muscles. An imbalance can lead to tight hip flexors and anterior pelvic tilt, which can lead to lower back pain or injury.

Gym Hygiene
- Understand how to fail safely as there is no need for spotters.
- Ensure the lifting area is free from obstacles such as unused weight plates and gym equipment.
- Full-size bumper weights should be used when lifting from the floor, anything smaller in diameter will increase stress on the lower back.

Set-Up
- The set-up position for the RDL will be the same as the 'Set-Up' and 'Ascent' section of the deadlift page (*see* 'Deadlift' section), however there will be a variation in the

Fig. 13.11 Romanian deadlift – start/finish position.

EXERCISE TECHNIQUE

execution of the lift. Typically, the athlete will perform a traditional deadlift to get the bar in the correct position to begin the execution of the RDL.
- The athlete should be standing upright with the bar around mid-thigh to hip crease and weight distribution should be in the mid-foot.
- The knees should be slightly flexed at an angle of approximately 15–20 degrees. Too much knee flexion and the exercise will not target hamstrings effectively and too little, the exercise will be a stiff-legged deadlift. If performed incorrectly the stiff-legged deadlift can potentially lead to spinal flexion under load and could pose an injury risk to an untrained athlete.
- The chest should be up, with the chin slightly tucked in and the neck in a neutral alignment with the rest of the upper body.

Descent
- Take a deep breath and hold.
- Initiate the movement by pushing the hips back (imagine closing a door behind you with your hips) whilst maintaining a neutral spine and braced trunk.
- The athlete should feel tension in the hamstrings throughout the descent.
- The weight distribution should shift from mid-foot to the heels.
- The bottom of the descent has been reached when either the athlete's back is parallel to the floor or the athlete's lower back begins to round. The athlete should not descend any further if the lower back is beginning to round, due to the injury risk to the lumbar spine. The bar will typically reach the bottom of the lift below the knee on the shins.
- The knee angle should remain constant throughout the descent.
- The bar should move down and slightly backwards and should be in contact/near contact with the body throughout the lift.
- Bar speed should be controlled during the descent at a speed where the athlete can maintain position.

Fig. 13.12 Romanian deadlift – bottom of descent position.

EXERCISE TECHNIQUE

Table 13.3 Romanian deadlift common faults

Common Fault	Technical Points	Coaching Points	Corrective Exercises
Flexed spine	Reduce the load	Brace the trunk	Posterior Chain Strength Exercises: Hip Thrusts (see Hip Thrust technical model), Good Morning (see Good Morning technical model)
	Scapula set back and down	Scapula back and down	Upper Back Strength Exercises: Bench Pull (see Bench Pull technical model) Pull Ups, Seated Row
	Are the athlete's legs straight or slightly flexed?	Descent in a controlled manner	Flat Back Feedback: RDL with wooden dowel placed on spine
	Does the athlete have enough mobility around the hips?	Push the hips away	Trunk Strength Exercises: Barbell Rollouts, Eleknas
Bar drifts away from body		Keep the bar close to the body Don't get too deep	RDL with object/wall behind athlete to encourage pushing hips away
	Reduce the load	Pull the bar to the body	Posterior Chain Strength Exercises: Deadlift (see Deadlift technical model), Good Morning (see Good Morning technical model), Hip Thrust (see Hip Thrust technical model)
	Does the athlete have the correct knee angle (too straight/too flexed)?	Shift the weight to the heels	
	Are the shoulders above the bar in the start position?	Keep the knees slightly bent	Back Strength Exercises: Bench Pull (see Bench Pull technical model), Pull Ups, Seated Row
	Does the athlete push the hips away from the body?	Push the hips away	Trunk Strength Exercises: Barbell Rollouts, Eleknas
	Reduce the load	Keep knees slightly bent and don't change the knee angle throughout lift	Posterior Chain Strength Exercises: Good Morning (see Good Morning technical model), Hip Thrust (see Hip Thrust technical model)
Large knee flexion on descent	Is the weight distribution at the midfoot or heels?	Feel tension in hamstrings not in the quadriceps	Hamstring Mobility
	Is the athlete offloading an injury?		
	Does the athlete have poor hip hamstring mobility?		

EXERCISE TECHNIQUE

Ascent
- The athlete should complete the descent in reverse, with the movement initiated from the hips with an aggressive hip extension movement, whilst maintaining a neutral spine and braced trunk.
- The athlete can return the bar to the floor in the same manner as the set-up but in reverse.
- Alternatively, drop the bar at the top of the ascent.

Corrective Exercise: Hip Thrust

Gym Hygiene
- Understand how to fail safely as there is no need for spotters.
- Ensure the lifting area is free from obstacles such as unused weight plates and gym equipment.
- Full-size bumper weights should be used when lifting from the floor, anything smaller in diameter will increase stress on the lower back.

Set-Up
- A hip thrust bench is the optimal piece of equipment to use for this exercise, however a weights bench or box will be suitable if at the correct height. Typically, height should be around 40cm (ranging from 33–48cm), however taller individuals may feel more comfortable with a higher bench. The athlete's hips should be parallel to the floor in full hip extension at the top position of the lift.
- Point of contact on the bench should be in a comfortable position around the bottom of the shoulder blades. The athlete might need to slightly re-adjust after a few repetitions to find a comfortable position.
- Roll the bar over the body to the crease of the hips, with the hands holding the bar in position to ensure it doesn't roll away and is aligned correctly in the middle of the hips. Hands should be in an overhand grip in a comfortable position wider than the hips. Use the markings on the bar to ensure symmetry of hand position.

Fig. 13.13 Hip thrust – start/finish position.

EXERCISE TECHNIQUE

Fig. 13.14 Hip thrust – top of the ascent position.

- Some athletes may not require padding on the bar, however it is recommended that the athlete protects the bony protrusions of the hips with something to make the exercise as comfortable as possible. An Airex® pad or yoga mat wrapped around the bar is usually suitable.
- Bring feet towards your hips and place the feet in a comfortable position around hip-width apart. Athletes can find a position that is comfortable for them, and typically athletes will adopt the same foot width and angle used for the back squat.
- Screw feet into the ground, so that when hips are fully extended the shins are vertical.
- Head should be in a neutral position with the chin slightly tucked throughout the lift.

Ascent
- The thrust should be completed in a smooth and fluid motion and not jerked off the floor.
- Take a deep breath in and hold.

- Initiate the movement by driving into the floor through the mid-foot and aggressively driving the hips vertically.
- During the ascent the knees should track along the line of the toes.
- The spine should remain in a neutral position throughout the lift, and the athlete should focus on only extending through the hips and not through the spine.
- The top of the ascent is reached when the hips are fully extended with a neutral spine. The torso should be parallel to the ground.
- Finish the ascent by contracting the gluteals hard in this top position to achieve full hip extension.

Descent
- The athlete should complete the ascent in reverse, with the movement initiated from the hips and a controlled descent to the floor.
- The athlete can return the bar to the floor in the same manner as the set-up but in reverse.

EXERCISE TECHNIQUE

BENCH PULL

Exercise Objective

The bench pull is the primary upper body strength exercise used in rowing. The bench pull will predominantly develop strength qualities around the posterior shoulder and back. The key muscles that the bench pull utilizes are the latissimus dorsi, trapezius, rhomboids, posterior deltoids and biceps.

Relation to Rowing

The bench pull supports the rowing stroke as it can develop the strength qualities required in the upper back to support the finish of the drive phase. It also develops back strength to support overall stability around the shoulders and suspension of the body throughout the drive phase.

Gym Hygiene
- Understanding how to bench pull safely is essential, including how to fail a lift without injury.
- Pay careful attention to how each bench pull can be adjusted to de-rack and rack the bar safely.
- Ensure the lifting area is free from obstacles such as unused weight plates and gym equipment.

Fig. 13.15 Bench pull – start/finish position.

EXERCISE TECHNIQUE

Set-Up

- Lie on the bench face-down ensuring your head is supported by the bench or sits within the face hole provided on some benches.
- Use a partner to fix the legs to the bench (pressure below the knees). Legs that are not fixed allow for a greater lumbar extension by the legs flailing in the air (like a fish tail).
- If there is no partner, the athlete should straddle the legs around the bench and hook the feet underneath (like a breast-stroke kick) with around a 90 degree hip flexion.
- Take a grip of the bar wider than the width of the bench pull itself with an overhand grip (palms facing towards your feet).
- Once the bar is taken from the rack, the bar should hang perpendicular to the floor with arms long and extended.
- Set the shoulders by 'squeezing' the shoulder blades back and down while simultaneously 'bracing the trunk'.

Ascent

- Take a deep breath and hold throughout the ascent.
- Aggressively pull the bar to the bench, roughly in line with the bottom of the sternum. The bar should move in a vertical upwards manner with no swinging.

Fig. 13.16 Bench pull – top of ascent position.

EXERCISE TECHNIQUE

Table 13.4 Bench pull common faults

Common Fault	Technical Points	Coaching Points	Corrective Exercises
Bar not touching underside of the bench	Reduce the load Practise moving the bar aggressively Practise brining elbows inwards to the torso during the ascent Ensure grip width is correct Ensure the legs are fixed	Break the bar Be aggressive	Upper Back Strength Exercises: Supine Row (see Supine Row Technical Model), Seated Row, Bent Over Row, Pull Up
Hypertension of the back	Reduce the load Are the legs fixed down to prevent hypertension? Athlete to 'brace' the trunk throughout the left	Anchor the legs (with partner/hook legs around bench) Keep ascent smooth Keep trunk 'braced'	Upper Back Strength Exercises: Supine Row (see Supine Row Technical Model), Seated Row, Bent Over Row, Pull Up Trunk Strength Exercises: Barbell Rollouts, Elekenas
Bar pulled to stomach and not bottom of sternum	Reduce the load Practise bringing elbows inwards to torso during ascent Ensure bar is at a dead hang and perpendicular to the floor at start of lift	Hit sternum with the bar Pull bar in a vertical line Keep elbows tight during ascent	Upper Back Strength Exercises: Supine row (see Supine Row Technical Model), Seated Row, Bent Over Row, Pull Up

- The elbows should be kept tight and pulled toward the trunk of the athlete and not pushed outwards.
- The bar should make contact with the underside of the bench. Benches have different depths, but the recommended depth is between 5–7cm: any less, athletes will hyperextend through their back to gain the extra range; any more, the athlete loses the strength benefits of the exercise.
- The chest and the trunk must remain on the bench throughout the ascent.

Descent
- In a controlled manner return the bar to the start position by allowing the elbows to extend. Don't let the bar drop in an uncontrolled manner.
- The bar should be lowered so that the arms are long and perpendicular to the floor.
- The chest and the trunk should remain in contact with the bench throughout the descent.
- Exhale from previous deep breath when the bar is returned and inhale again in preparation for the next repetition.

Re-Racking
- In a controlled manner, slowly return the bar to the rack until you hear contact of the bar with the rack.
- Slowly lower the bar into the rack.
- If there is no rack, drop the bar onto the floor after it has been lowered in a controlled manner.

Corrective Exercise: Supine Row

Gym Hygiene
- Understanding how to set up and complete a supine row safely is essential.
- Pay careful attention to how each supine row can be set up using a suspension system.
- Ensure the lifting area is free from obstacles such as unused weight plates and gym equipment.

Set-Up
- Adopt a lying position directly under the suspension system, which is vertical and in line with the shoulders.
- Knees should be flexed, and feet should be planted firmly on the ground hip-width apart, tight to the hips.
- Arms are positioned in a vertical position, so the fingertips can touch the bottom of the handles.
- Palms hold the handles in a neutral grip and scapulae should be pulled back and down.
- When shoulder blades have been retracted, the athlete should simultaneously brace the trunk and lift the hips, so the body is lifted from the ground.

Ascent
- Take a deep breath and hold throughout the ascent.
- Smoothly raise the body under control and bring the handles tight into the side of the body so the hands are in line with the lower chest.
- Hands must be in a hammer-grip position with palms facing each other throughout the ascent.
- The head should remain in a neutral position and the athlete should maintain alignment of the spine.
- The top of the ascent has been reached when the hands are in line with the chest.

Descent
- In a controlled manner, fully extend the elbows and lower back to the start position.
- Athletes must maintain body alignment through the descent.

EXERCISE TECHNIQUE

Fig. 13.17 Supine row – start/finish position.

EXERCISE TECHNIQUE

Fig. 13.18 Supine row – top of the ascent position.

EXERCISE TECHNIQUE

Fig. 13.22 Press up – bottom of descent position.

- The arms should be fully extended, and the body should be aligned from head to ankle in the top position.
- Exhale from previous deep breath and inhale again in preparation for the next repetition.

CONCLUSION

Having technical models of weightlifting exercises provides the coach with a reference point to assess how a rower is lifting against these models. Without these models of what excellence should look like, it is almost impossible to determine what good looks like and how a rower is performing against this. When a rower is weightlifting, the question 'Is this perfect technique?' should be asked. If the answer is no, the following questions should be explored:

- What is stopping the rower from performing the exercise with perfect technique?
- What can be done to help the rower to lift with perfect technique?

These two questions provide a basis of exercise modulation using the corrective exercises, coaching and technical points available within this chapter.

It is important to note there are many training methods and techniques to help rowers lift more effectively. This is by no means a definitive guide, nor are these the only technical models available. These are, however, technical models that have been effective in supporting rowers to become more technically proficient in the weight room. The exercises provided are ones that are commonly prescribed to rowers. This is not a definitive list and many other exercises will be used, but this chapter will provide the basis for the majority of training programmes for rowers.

REFERENCES

1. Pritchard, J. (2012). *Pavlova: Twentieth Century Ballerina.* Bergamo, Italy: Castelli Bolis Poligrafiche S.p.A.
2. Rippetoe, M. (2011). *Starting Strength: Basic Barbell Training.* Texas, USA: The Aasgaard Company.
3. Thompson, P., & Wolf, A. (2015). *Training for the Complete Rower: A guide to improving your performance.* Wiltshire, UK: The Crowood Press.

14 TRUNK-TRAINING

A chain is only as strong as its weakest link
Thomas Reid[1]

INTRODUCTION

Injuries that place significant demands on the spine through repetitive and intensive directional loading are common in sports such as rowing.[2,3,4] There is a high prevalence of spinal injuries within rowing populations, with one study suggesting nearly a third of all injuries reported in international rowers were related to the lumbar spine.[5] Strategies to manage injury risk and enhance spinal function are a priority to ensure firstly the health of the rower, and secondly reduce the amount of time lost in training from injury. Spinal function has been defined as 'the ability to create, absorb, and transfer force and motion to the terminal appendicular segments during the performance of skilled motor tasks'.[6] When analysing the rowing stroke at a basic level, the spine of a rower is required to maintain spinal integrity under a variety of loads and motion demands, as it must be able to create, absorb and transfer large forces from the legs in the drive phase to the arms in the finish, to ensure a forceful, smooth and efficient rowing stroke. Greater understanding of the rowing stroke can be found in *Training for the Complete Rower: A guide to improving your performance.*[7]

Spinal function is integral within rowing and this is reflected within land training practices across the sport. However, from personal experience of working across a diverse range of sports and athletes, spinal exercise prescription is often described by the name, place performed or by the equipment used (for example mat exercises, Pilates, stability ball core training). As previously described in Chapters 4 to 9, this does not provide enough clarity of the intended outcome, only the method employed. Instead, the intention, execution and loading of the exercise should be identified to fully support the rower's performance development requirements.[8]

Traditionally within rowing, this type of training has been termed 'core' or 'core stability training' which has been defined as 'the ability to control the position and motion of the trunk over the pelvis and leg'.[9] This typically refers to the stabilizing system of the small, local muscles that provide segmental stability while the global system refers to muscles that enable trunk movement during more demanding tasks.[10] In the past, core stability has been a popular tool in manage-

TRUNK-TRAINING

ment of chronic low back pain.[11] However, this term creates uncertainty, as it is often used to achieve multiple training outcomes and it does not define the intent of the exercise. Research completed by clinicians in recent years has led to a deeper understanding on the relationship between the complex coordination between the neuromuscular system and passive anatomical structures, as opposed to the traditional approach of training isolated groups of core muscles.

This chapter will provide a framework for spinal exercise prescription that clearly defines the nature of the prescription required to deliver the intended physical outcomes, and how this framework is implemented within rowing. Spinal training will be termed trunk-training from this point on. The framework is taken from the co-authored article by Spencer et al.[12] where spinal exercises were classified based on the exercise objective alongside the intended physical outcome. Additionally, these exercises can be further sub-classified by spinal displacement (static or dynamic), function (functional or non-functional) and intended physical outcome (motor control, work capacity and strength). To better understand this and how it applies to rowing, these areas will be explored further.

SPINAL DISPLACEMENT

During movement tasks, the spine will be involved in one of two ways. First the spine can provide a static platform whereby the spine remains in an unaltered position and the appendages (legs and arms) move around the spine: this can be termed segmental stabilization. An example of this would be the spine during the rowing stroke (Figs 14.1–14.3). Stiffening strategies are coordinated by the neuromuscular system to provide this static platform.

Figs 14.1, 14.2, and 14.3 Sequence of rowing stroke (spine providing a static platform).

many months that creates a chronic adaptation to sustain repeated and variable loading.[21] Work capacity is vital for the rower to be able to repeatedly transfer, absorb and dissipate repeated submaximal forces. During the rowing stroke the trunk musculature keeps the spine rigid during high forces generated by the legs, the trunk forms part of the kinetic chain and allows these forces to be transferred onto the oar. The trunk must be capable of doing this repeatedly during every rowing stroke. Additionally, research shows that reductions in trunk muscular endurance as well as changes in endurance ratios are a risk factor for injuries and have been identified in people with lower back pain.[22] Chapter 9 gives a thorough overview of work capacity and how it can be applied to rowing populations.

Strength

Within the Spencer *et al.* article[23], strength has been split into two areas, maximal force expression and rate of force development. These definitions are identical to maximal force expression and rate of force development definitions in Chapters 6 and 7, respectively. Maximal force expression can be defined as the musculature's ability to produce the greatest magnitude of force.[24] Rate of force development (RFD) is time-dependent and can be defined as the rate of the rise of contractile forces at the start of a muscle action.[25] Trunk strength is an important physical quality to develop. For greater understanding around this quality and the wider model of trunk-training, reading this article in full is suggested.

RELATIONSHIP TO ROWERS

As described in the sections above, there is clear rationale why some trunk-training exercises and methods would be biased over others. From a spinal displacement perspective, most of the trunk-training for rowers should be biased around segmental stabilization. Chapter 11 examines common injuries within rowing populations including potential mechanisms. This helps to define why non-functional exercises are most likely to be biased within a rowing population. The ability to target specific musculature around the trunk and hip will support both the rower's trunk health and its performance during the rowing stroke with the potential to limit the time lost out of the boat through pain and injury. Due to the demands of rowing both in terms of the repetitive nature of the rowing stroke and the large overall training volume, work-capacity based trunk-training should be a staple for all rowers. This type of training will provide a significant opportunity for the trunk to adapt to the demands of the sport. If a decision had to be made around what type of trunk-training should be prioritized for rowers, non-functional segmental stabilization work capacity exercises would be the priority.

BUILDING A TRUNK-TRAINING PROGRAMME

Prior to working within rowing programmes or with rowers, a simple method to firstly assess then prescribe trunk training exercises based on the assessments was developed to support working with athletes across several sports. This has been found to be hugely successful in making significant changes with the vast majority of athletes who have used this method. The assessment and prescription are biased towards non-functional segmental stabilization work capacity making it a highly relevant method for rowers.

Trunk Assessment

The trunk is split into four quadrants: anterior

TRUNK-TRAINING

Prone extension

Fig. 14.8 Prone extension test position.

Fig. 14.9 Prone extension common fault – hyperextension.

Fig. 14.10 Prone extension common fault – loss of shoulder and hip alignment.

TRUNK-TRAINING

Supine hold

Start Position	• Lie face down with feet together and ASIS on edge of box • Tester or partner sits across lower legs below the knee to support athlete • Use a mat for comfort if necessary • Arms are folded across the chest • Head, neck and shoulders in neutral position • The trunk is parallel to the floor – shoulders in line with hips • Start timing once the athlete is in the correct postural position
Assessment Rules	• Shoulders remain in line with hips • Neutral to slightly flexed back position • Head remains in neutral
Gross Movement Deviations	• Significant drop of shoulders below hips • Significant flexion of the mid-back and shoulders • Head position significantly deviates away from neutral
Benchmark Time	• 120 seconds (test terminated at 140 seconds)

Fig. 14.11 Supine hold assessment set-up.

Fig. 14.12 Supine hold test position.

TRUNK-TRAINING

Fig. 14.13 Supine hold common fault – significant flexion of the mid-back and shoulders.

Fig. 14.14 Supine hold common fault – significant drop of shoulders below hip height.

TRUNK-TRAINING

Lateral Hold

Start Position	• Lie sideways on box with body fully extended with ASIS on the edge of the box • Place top leg slightly behind bottom • Tester or partner sits across lower legs below the knee to support athlete • Fold arms across the chest and maintain a neutral posture • Neck in neutral position • The trunk is parallel to the floor • Start timing once the athlete is in the correct postural position
Assessment Rules	• Top hip stays above bottom hip • Top shoulder stays above bottom shoulder • Maintain 'square' trunk position with shoulders in line with hips • Shoulders remain at same height as hips ***NOTE: When the rower is lying on their left hip, the assessment is testing the right lateral trunk and vice versa***
Gross Movement Deviations	• Significant drop in shoulder height below hips • Significant increase in shoulder height above the hips • Rotation of the trunk
Benchmark Time	• 180 seconds (test terminated at 200 seconds)

Fig. 14.15 Lateral hold assessment set-up.

Fig. 14.16 Lateral hold test position.

TRUNK-TRAINING

Fig. 14.17 Lateral hold common fault – significant drop in shoulder height below the hips.

Fig. 14.18 Lateral hold common fault – rotation of the trunk.

TRUNK-TRAINING

WRITING A TRUNK-TRAINING PROGRAMME

Based upon the assessment times a rower achieves, a training programme can be prescribed with a greater focus on the quadrants with the lowest scores. Table 14.1 outlines the standards for each quadrant. These will help determine the focus and time required to spend on each of the four quadrants.

The standards are broken down into several levels: excellent, average and poor. There is an expectation that all adult rowers should be able to reach the excellent level with consistent training. Those who can reach 'excellent' are more likely to be able to tolerate the training load within the programme and may have a better resistance to trunk or spine pain and injury. It is important that the assessment data is saved so that progressions can be tracked, and training programmes altered accordingly. A change of 15 seconds has been identified as meaningful. So, if a rower produces a time greater or less than 15 seconds of the previous assessment, there is confidence that this is a worthwhile change. If the current assessment time is within 15 seconds of the previous assessment, there is a strong chance the rower has not made a meaningful change. If a rower is unfortunate enough to receive a spine or trunk injury, the saved data will provide a guide of where the rower needs to return to or exceed with regards to these assessments. This has been a fundamental part of helping rowers return to full training post-injury.

Trunk-Training Prescription

After an assessment, each quadrant can be placed within the standards from Table 14.1. Assessment scores that are excellent are denoted in green, average in yellow and poor in red. Greater focus should be given to the quadrants that fall within the poor standard, followed by those that fall within average

Table 14.1 Trunk quadrant assessment standards

Standard	Prone Extension (seconds)	Supine Hold (seconds)	Lateral Trunk Hold (seconds)
Excellent	≥180	≥120	≥180
Average	150	90	150
Poor	≤120	≤60	≤120
Meaningful Change	15	15	15

and least focus on those that fall within the excellent standard. The eventual goal within this trunk-training method is to have equality across all four quadrants within the excellent standard.

The basic framework is to create an 8-minute trunk circuit consisting of 16 x 30-second blocks of work. Each of the blocks of work will be assigned to a trunk quadrant. The quadrant with poorer assessment times will utilize more of these 30-second blocks while the quadrants with greater assessment times will use less of them. The distribution of how many of these blocks of work are used by each quadrant can be established using Fig. 14.19.

Fig. 14.19 highlights every possible combination of trunk composition based on a quadrant's assessment score in relation to the other three quadrants. This is denoted by the red, yellow and green colours aligned to the standards identified in Table 14.1. For example, if all four quadrant assessment times fall within the same standard, each quadrant will have four blocks of 30-seconds work (2 minutes total per quadrant), totalling 8 minutes. If each quadrant has a different assessment standard, the distribution of 30-second blocks of work will vary.

Fig. 14.19 highlights the number of blocks of work that should be prescribed based on these variations. The colours used coordinate with the standards in Table 14.1, which

TRUNK-TRAINING

4	4	4	4

4–5 per quadrant totalling 13	3

4–5 per quadrant totalling 10	6

5	5	3	3

4	4	4	2

4	4	4	4

4–5 per quadrant totalling 14	3

3	3	3	7

6	6	2	2

5	5	4	2

4	4	4	4

4–5 per quadrant totalling 13	3

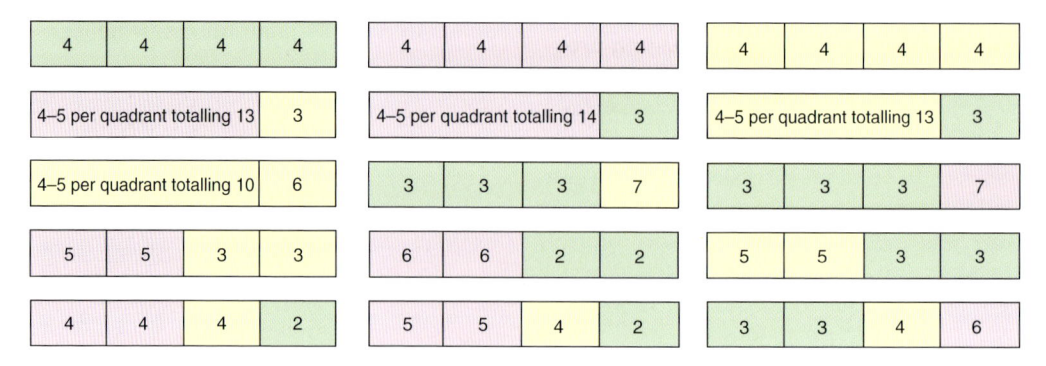

3	3	3	7

5	5	3	3

3	3	4	6

Fig. 14.19 Trunk composition based on quadrant assessments.

allows for easier cross-referencing between the standard and the number of blocks of work. Each possible combination of quadrant standard will have a series of numbers within the boxes. This dictates the number of blocks of work that should be completed for that quadrant within the 8-minute circuit. Using this framework aligned to the assessments, it is now possible to prescribe an individual trunk-training programme based on the bespoke needs of each rower.

Trunk-Training Programming Examples

Table 14.2 highlights assessment results of two rowers. Based on the guidelines above, it is possible to determine how to construct a trunk-training programme using the assessment results.

Rower A has reached the prone extension standard with 200 seconds, the average standard with both left and right lateral hold and the poor standard for the supine hold. Based

4	4	6	2

Fig. 14.20 Rower A's trunk composition distribution.

on Rower A results, Fig. 14.20 highlights the trunk composition distribution.

The distribution of trunk-training for Rower A is highlighted in Table 14.3. The programme highlights the distribution of the different training focusing on a specific quadrant of the trunk. This also provides clarity to the rower and support team on what the focus of training is and where the bias of loading is occurring.

Fig. 14.21 and Table 14.4 are Rower B's trunk composition distribution and training programme respectively. While the bias of quadrant training is different to Rower A, there is still clarity on the focus on training specific to the individual rower's needs.

4–5 per quadrant totalling 13	3

Fig. 14.21 Rower B's trunk composition distribution.

Table 14.2 Trunk quadrant assessment standards

Rower	Prone Extension (seconds)	Supine Hold (seconds)	Lateral Trunk Hold (seconds)	Right Lateral Hold
A	200	112	158	164
B	154	115	100	93

Table 14.3 Rower A's trunk-training programme

Exercise Number	Quadrant	Exercise	Time (seconds)
1	Anterior	Front plank	30
2	Left Lateral	Left side plank	30
3	Right Lateral	Right side plank	30
4	Anterior	Swiss ball roll out	30
5	Left Lateral	Weighted lateral hold – left	30
6	Right Lateral	Weighted lateral hold – right	30
7	Anterior	Front plank	30
8	Posterior	Weighted prone extension	30
9	Anterior	Swiss ball roll out	30
10	Left Lateral	Left side plank	30
11	Right Lateral	Right side plank	30
12	Anterior	Front plank	30
13	Left Lateral	Weighted lateral hold – left	30
14	Right Lateral	Weighted lateral hold – right	30
15	Anterior	Swiss ball roll out	30
16	Posterior	Weighted prone extension	30

Total: 8 minutes

Table 14.4 Rower B's trunk-training programme

Exercise Number	Quadrant	Exercise	Time (seconds)
1	Anterior	Front plank	30
2	Left Lateral	Left plank	30
3	Right Lateral	Right plank	30
4	Posterior	Prone extension	30
5	Anterior	Swiss ball roll out	30
6	Left Lateral	Lateral hold – left	30
7	Right Lateral	Lateral hold – right	30
8	Posterior	Prone extension	30
9	Anterior	Front plank	30
10	Left Lateral	Left plank	30
11	Right Lateral	Right plank	30
12	Anterior	Swiss ball roll out	30
13	Left Lateral	Lateral hold – left	30
14	Right Lateral	Lateral hold – right	30
15	Anterior	Front plank	30
16	Posterior	Prone extension	30

Total: 8 minutes

CONCLUSION

This can be a very effective method of developing the trunk work capacity of rowers. The beauty of it is the ability to individualize training programmes for each and every rower focusing attention on the areas that need the greatest amount of work. Secondly it is evidence-based, as the programming is prescribed from the assessment results. This will allow the continued adjustment to the programme to meet the needs of the rower throughout the season through periodic assessment. With the standards identified, it also provides rowers with the opportunity to continually target the next progression. Because the assessments are capped, it also means once rowers have attained the excellent standard, there is no need to develop this any further: it is a case of maintaining that standard. It is also worth noting that when trunk quadrants are biased with a greater number of blocks of work, this automatically reduces the number of blocks of work for the quadrants that have better assessment results.

Originally, there was concern that these quadrants would start to have a decline in the work capacity as identified through the assessments. However, this has not been the case with a single healthy and injury-free rower. Rowers have maintained the work capacity of the quadrants that are not trained with as many blocks of work. The hypothesis is that because all the musculature around the trunk regardless of quadrant is interconnected, biasing the loading of one quadrant will have a secondary effect of loading the remaining quadrants – albeit not to the same degree, but enough to maintain or make the necessary improvements. As stated earlier in the chapter, if there was a need to prioritize trunk-training, it would be this methodology due to its ease and effectiveness at making significant changes at an individual rower level.

REFERENCES

1. Reid, T. (2012). *Essays on the Intellectual Powers of Man (Classic Reprint)*. London, UK: Forgotten Books.
2. McGregor, A. H., Anderton, L., & Gedroyc, W. M. W. (2002). The Trunk Muscles of Elite Oarsmen. *British Journal of Sports Medicine*. 36, 214–17.
3. Thornton, J. S., Vinther, A., Wilson, F., Lebrun, C. M., Wilkinson, M., Di Ciacca, S. R., Orlando, K., & Smoljanovic, T. (2016). Rowing Injuries: An Updated Review. *Sports Medicine*. 47, 641–61.
4. Wilson, F., Gissane, C., Gormley, J., & Simms, C. (2010). A 12-Month Prospective Cohort Study of Injury in International Rowers. *British Journal of Sports Medicine*. 44, 207–14.
5. *Ibid.*
6. Spencer, S., Wolf, A., & Rushton, A. (2016). Spinal-Exercise Prescription in Sport: Classifying Physical Training and Rehabilitation by Intention and Outcome. *Journal of Athletic Training*. 51, 613–28.
7. Thompson, P., & Wolf, A. (2015). *Training for the Complete Rower: A guide to improving your performance*. Wiltshire, UK: The Crowood Press.
8. Spencer *et al.* (2016).
9. Kibler, W.B., Press, J., & Sciascia, A. (2006). The Role of Core Stability in Athletic Function. *Sports Medicine*. 36, 189–98.
10. *Ibid.*
11. Hodges, P. W. (2003). Core Stability Exercise in Chronic Low Back Pain. *Orthopedic Clinics of North America*. 34, 245–54.
12. Spencer *et al.* (2016).
13. *Ibid.*
14. Boyle, M. (2010). *Advances in Functional Training: Training Techniques for Coaches, Personal Trainers and Athletes*. Aptos, CA: On Target Publications.
15. Spencer *et al.* (2016).
16. Tsao, H., & Hodges, P. W. (2008). Persistence of Improvements in Postural Strategies Following Motor Control Training

in People with Recurrent Low Back Pain. *Journal of Electromyography & Kinesiology.* 18, 559–67.
17. Spencer *et al.* (2016).
18. Hodges (2003).
19. Spencer *et al.* (2016).
20. Ibid.
21. Ibid.
22. Jones, M. A., Stratton, G., Reilly, T., & Unnithan, V. B. (2005). Biological Risk Indicators for Recurrent Non-Specific Low Back Pain in Adolescents. *British Journal of Sports Medicine.* 39, 137–40.
23. Spencer *et al.* (2016).
24. Stone, M. H., Sands, W. A., Carlock, J., Callan, S., Dickie, D., Daigle, K., Cotton, J., Smith, S. L., & Hartman, H. (2004). The Importance of Isometric Maximum Strength and Peak Rate-of-Force Development in Sprint Cycling. *Journal of Strength and Conditioning Research.* 18, 878–84.
25. Aagaard, P., Simonsen, E. B., Andersen, J. L., Magnusson, P., & Dyhre-Poulsen, P. (2002). Increased Rate of Force Development and Neural Drive of Human Skeletal Muscle Following Resistance Training. *Journal of Applied Physiology,* 93, 1,318–26.

CONCLUSION

Reasoning draws a conclusion... but does not make the conclusion certain... unless the mind discovers it by the path of experience

Roger Bacon[1]

I stated at the beginning of the book the desire to bring to life some of the areas within S&C which I felt were important but often overlooked, or not enough attention is placed upon them in texts and education programmes. The early chapters give perspectives of both rowing coaches and rowers that provide probably the most important insights of why we as S&C coaches do what we do. The coach's perspective provides a strong validation for S&C to be truly unified to the wider performance needs of the rowers, including understanding the coach's model of performance. There is a shared, agreed and understood performance plan for each rower. This clearly articulates how each component part and discipline's service align to the overarching plan, so that all those supporting the rowers are collaboratively contributing to their success. The single biggest failure of S&C is viewing it in isolation to the rest of the programme and judging success on what happens in the weight room. S&C is not the event itself. Truly great things can happen when a performance support team collaboratively problem-solve together.

The rowers' perspectives in Chapter 2 provide a poignant and often neglected point. Rowers are people too and face the same challenges and pitfalls as every other person in the world. Never underestimate the impact you can have on an individual by the way you interact with them. The effect will be far wider reaching than you may imagine and may not be for what you are probably employed to do. As Carl Buehner said, 'They may forget what you said – but they will never forget how you made them feel'.[2] How do you want the athletes you work with to feel when being coached by you? Alternatively, what experience do you want the athletes you work with to have? I am certain if you have these questions in the back of your mind when you are coaching, you won't go far wrong.

Understanding the performance needs and the demands of racing on rowers is an area we think we mostly get right. Some of the early chapters remind us of the idea of performance backwards. What are the component parts that contribute to performance and how are we as S&C coaches able to support this? Looking from the performance backwards approach ensures the intended outcome is

CONCLUSION

the focus and not the methods used. It is easy to work from first principles and assume that if rowers are more forceful and explosive, this will translate into moving a boat faster. It is also easy to continue to use training methodologies or exercise selections based on our historical use and biases, and try to fit this into the needs of performance. However, working backwards from the performance needs requires a greater depth of critical thinking and problem solving to determine the best methods to affect the performance needs. It may be harder but is undoubtedly more effective than the very large leaps of faith in assuming first principles will impact performance.

As stated in Chapter 5, there are many matrixes' ways to define training methods which can be found in pretty much any S&C text. The premise for providing the one in this book is to start with the intended outcome first and work backwards. Secondly it is used in an attempt to clean up the terminology of how we describe strength-training methods. Strength training is not an outcome; it is a training method. Defining the outcome first gives us clarity on what we want to change and then how we may go about doing this. This is the biggest (and maybe the only) difference this matrix has to others. This has helped provide me and the S&C coaches I have worked alongside with greater clarity on what we are really trying to change. It creates a cleaner reference point to anchor discussions around training as we all mean the same thing when we talk about 'maximal force expression' or any other of the adaptive responses included. To help with being specific with the adaptive response or the training methods used, try banning several words that are liberally used to describe a multitude of things. These include strength, power, fit/fitter, strong/stronger, robust and healthy. How will you describe the change if you cannot use the word 'stronger'? You must be more specific and articulate what is your intended outcome.

The final few chapters provide insight around common exercises used by rowers and some of the trunk-training methods used. This is in no way an exhaustive list but demonstrates exercises and methods that are most useful for rowers. This does not mean every rower needs to do these or that if rowers are not doing these, they will not progress. Using the content and principles of the rest of the book will allow rowers to use whatever exercises are most practical for their personal needs. Not everyone needs to back squat or deadlift but referring to Chapters 4 and 5, and the paragraph above, work out what the intended outcome is and then define exercise selection thereafter. The trunk-training method shared in Chapter 14 is something I have found useful for all athletes I have worked with over the last fifteen years and originated outside of rowing. It has been a useful tool to focus rowers' attention on a concentrated amount of trunk work and has been very successful in making significant changes with its use.

When I have been very specific with what I am looking to change and able to articulate this, the types of training and methods used become almost infinite. This is because there is real clarity of change required, therefore the manipulation of training to attain this becomes easier. However the less specific I am, the more vague the outcome is, which reduces the number of methods or exercise selection. This is because only certain methods and exercises are possible to cover several different but related outcomes. For example, if the goal is to develop maximal concentric force expression of the knee extenders, there are many ways to do this. If I state I need to develop maximal strength of the legs, there are only a few exercises or methods that allow me to develop the maximal strength of the entire leg musculature. This is limiting and can easily be avoided.

Secondly, a lot of what is written in this book may come across as definitive and may feel like there is real certainty to what is being shared. It is worth noting that everything we do has a

CONCLUSION

degree of uncertainty and there are no definitive answers – anyone that tells you otherwise may not be entirely reliable. I tend to look at this as a series of stepping stones in terms of everything we do is a leap of faith to a certain degree. There are some stones that are easily stepped across. These are things we are a lot more certain about, such as heavy strength training will most likely improve maximal force expression. Our observations and testing give us a high degree of certainty around this. Then there are stones that we must stretch to. These are things like naming the exact adaptive responses stimulated during heavy strength training. We think we know them, but we have no real way of specifically defining these. The final stones are those we must take big leaps to get across. This could include stating heavy strength training can help manage the risk of spinal and hip injuries in rowers. There is no way this can be assessed nor are we certain that this is the case. It is a hypothesis we may never be able to test but there are casual relationships that may be observed with the rowers. None of these are good or bad, they are what they are. The important bit is to recognize when something is a step, a stretch or a leap, be comfortable with what it is and not try to pass it off as something else. It is OK to work in uncertainty; it keeps us evolving the work we do. When we gravitate to certainty, we are holding on to a false sense of security which will at some point tumble and expose us to the real complexity of what we are dealing with.

Finally, the later chapters in the book have been an enjoyable process of pulling together thoughts and experiences and discussing topics with several people who have given support. However, the conclusion has been a little trickier. It is one of the shortest sections of the book and should bring all the chapters together as if some final act on the stage! This is what I struggled most with – thinking of this as the end. The quote from Roger Bacon at the start of the conclusion sums up the sentiment and feeling nicely.

This is certainly not the end, merely the interpretation of my experiences at this current point in time. I am certain that this collective understanding will evolve as I am exposed to infinite novel experiences ahead. This book has provided an opportunity for me to formulate and write down in a coherent manner what is often left swimming in my head. This has given me greater clarity or at the very least a better articulation of why I do what I do and what is important to me. My ambition is that this book in some way facilitates the build on your current knowledge and experiences.

In the book *The Conquest of Happiness*, Bertrand Russell writes 'events only become experiences through the interest we take in them'.[3] What has been shared in this book are my and the contributors' experiences and the interpretation we have given them to inform our decision-making. It is more than possible that you may disagree with some of the content. This is equally as useful to those who agree or helps build on existing thought process and decision-making. As Walt Whitman, the American poet and journalist said, 'Be curious, not judgmental'.[4] I started this book inviting you to be inquisitive and to ask questions. If you disagree with any of the content, what is the reasoning and where and how does this differ to your thought process? If you agree, what has given you greater clarity or understanding? If any of the content has helped build on your existing thought process and decision-making, what are the connections and how are they linked? Learning has acquisition and application elements.

If this book is in some way the acquisition part, the final questions are what can you and what will you do differently tomorrow?

REFERENCES

1. Evans, R. (1984). *Richard Evans' Quote Book*. Utah, USA: Publishers Press.
2. *Ibid.*

3. Russell, B. (2013). *The Conquest of Happiness*. New York, USA: Liveright Publishing Corporation.
4. Walt Whitman Quotes. (n.d.). BrainyQuote.com. Retrieved November 8, 2019, from BrainyQuote.com Website: https://www.brainyquote.com/quotes/walt_whitman_146892

INDEX

adaption-led training 41
adductor group 66–8, 113
adductor magnus 66–8
amortization phase 73–4
anthropometrics 83–4
arm injuries 103
arms, & rowing power 30
asymmetries & imbalances 94, 107–8

back injuries & problems 48–9, 72, 103, 106–11
back squat 61, 62–3, 121–3
   common faults 123
   objective 121
   & rowing 121
bench press 146–9
   common faults 148
   objective 146
   & rowing 146
bench pull 111, 140–5
   common faults 142
   objective 142
   & rowing 142
Bennett, Karen 24–5
bio-impedance measurements 84
Boddy, Chris 81–3
body-mass changes, measuring 83–4
box squat 122–7

calorie restriction, dangers 113
Carnegie-Brown, Olivia 25
catch position 30, 31, 38, 66, 101
causation, upward/downward 40–1
chest wall injuries 102, 103, 106, 111–13
circuit training 69–70
Collins, Dave 11
concentric muscle contraction 73–4
concurrent training 64–5, 86–7
co-ordination development 42
countermovement jump challenge 40–1
Coxless Crew, The 28

Dalio, Ray 59
deadlift 128–32
   common faults 132
   objective 128
   & rowing 128
distances, diversity of, in competition 29–30
drive & recovery 31, 73–4
dual energy X-ray absorptiometry (DEXA) 83

economy of strokes 30, 32
elbow injuries 103
ergometers 30, 75, 116
event, demands of 29–30
evidence-based practice 19–20

INDEX

explosive strength training   72–3, 75–6
   & heavy strength training, mixed   76
extraction   31, 32

femoral acetabular impingement (FAI)   113
ForceDecks   75
front squat   127–8
functional training   48–50, 154–6

gluteus maximus   66
Good Morning   133–5
grip strength   68–9

hamstring exercises   108–11
high volume, low intensity training   94, 96
high/low repetition programmes   57–8
hip bridge, loaded   60
hip extension mechanism   66
hip injuries   103, 113
hip range movement   108
hip thrusts   110, 138–9
hip-based force   14
hypertrophy training   79

injuries/injury risk   48, 91, 94, 106–14
   lightweight rowers   111–13
   para-rowers   102
   & training intensity   114
insight approach   42–4
integration of training   32–3
intent, importance of   65

jump assessment   75

knee injuries   113–14
knee-based force   14

leadership
   characteristics   20–4
   emergent   21
lifting exercises   68–9
lifting, limiting factors   68–9
limb deficiency, & para-rowing   100
loads, raising   69–70
low volume, high intensity training   95, 96

machine weights, v barbell   48–9
maximal force expression training   48–50, 51–70, 90, 157
   & adductors   8
   assessing change   54–6
   & circuit training
   concurrent training   64–5
   & athletes' intent   65
   limiting factors   68–9
   load & capability of musculature   60
   most effective exercise   60–1
   principles   59–70
   programme guidelines   56–9
   regularity   61–2
   & rowing   54
   single limb training   68
   technique, importance   62
maximal handle force   31
Maximum Aerobic Speed (MAS)   63–4
moderate volume, moderate intensity training   94–5
motor control   156
muscle & tendon mass   48, 80–8
   assessing change   83
   case study   81–3
   concurrent training   86–7
   increasing   79–80
   programme guidelines   84–7
   & rowing performance   80–3

neck injuries   102–3
neurological disorders, & para-rowing   100
neuromuscular performance, outcome   46–50
Nichol, Cameron   28

optimal movement, achieving   37–9

Paralympics   98
   coaching for   104–5
para-rowing   98–105
   classification   98, 99
   impairments, understanding   99–100
   injury risks   102–3
   mechanical demands   100–2

175

INDEX

'performance backwards' approach   12–14, 81–2
performance support team, leading   15–17
Pickering, Stuart   20–1
plyometric tasks   73–4
power strokes   117–118
'power' training, incorrect term   72–3
press-ups   149–50
pullovers   111, 112

rate of force development (RDF)   48, 72–8, 157
   assessing change   74–5
   plyometric tasks   73–4
   programme guidelines   75–7
   regularity & frequency of training   77
   & rowing   73–4
regatta rowing   29–30
repetition maximum   55–6
retrospective coherence   36
rib cage, injury risk   91, 94, 111
Rio Olympics   29
Romanian Deadlift (RDL)   135–8
   common faults   137
   objective   135
   & rowing   135
rowers' perspectives   24–7
rowing
   mechanical demands   30–2
   popularity   28
   psychological dynamics   29–30
   strokes   13–14, 30
   WOD (workout of the day)   28
rowing coach/S&C coach relationship   17–18, 21–3

S&C coaching, fundamentals   19–27
shared understanding   36–8
single limb training   68
social capital   22–3
specific skill emergence   42
spinal cord injury, & para-rowing   99–100
spinal exercises   106–11, 151

spinal injuries   48–9, 72, 103, 106–11, 151
spinal loading   60
squats   61, 62–3, 120–8
stability/variability, balance between   38–9
starts, practising   118
strength, concepts of   46–7
stress removal   23
structural v neural changes   40
supine row   143–5
symmetry, tracking   93–4

Thompson, Paul   12–18
traditional exercises, alternatives   48–9
training
   as creative act   35–6
   insights tool   43
   transferring to performance   116–19
trunk   30, 38
   assessing   93, 157–64
   quadrants   157–8
trunk training   151–68
   assessment for   157–64
   creating training programme   165–8
   examples   166–7
   physical outcomes   156–7
   & rowing   157
   spinal displacement   152–4

velocity, measuring   77
Verkhoshansky, Prof. Yuri   63–4
visual impairment, & para-rowing   100, 104

water sprints   118–19
weighing   83
Wilson, Mel   25–6
work capacity
   assessing/monitoring change   92–4
   definition   89–90, 156–7
   exercise outcomes   156–7
   programme guidelines   94–6
   principles   96–7
   & rowing   90–2